THE
ABOLITIONIST
MOVEMENT

THE
ABOLITIONIST
MOVEMENT

AMERICAN
SOCIAL
MOVEMENTS

THE
ABOLITIONIST
MOVEMENT

James Tackach, *Book Editor*

Bruce Glassman, *Vice President*
Bonnie Szumski, *Publisher*
Helen Cothran, *Managing Editor*

GREENHAVEN PRESS
An imprint of Thomson Gale, a part of The Thomson Corporation

THOMSON

GALE

Detroit • New York • San Francisco • San Diego • New Haven, Conn.
Waterville, Maine • London • Munich

THOMSON
GALE

Cover credit: © akg-images. President Abraham Lincoln is depicted freeing the slaves. In 1863, Lincoln issued the Emancipation Proclamation, which freed slaves in the states rebelling against the Union.
Digital Stock, 165, 190
Dover Publications, 144
Library of Congress, 117
National Archives, 107, 151

LIBRARY OF CONGRESS CATALOGING-IN-PUBLICATION DATA

The abolitionist movement / James Tackach, book editor.
    p. cm. — (American social movements)
Includes bibliographical references and index.
ISBN 0-7377-1945-1 (lib. : alk. paper)
    1. Antislavery movements—United States—History—Sources. 2. Abolitionists—United States—History—Sources. 3. Slavery—United States—History—Sources.
I. Tackach, James. II. Series.
E441.A26 2005
326'.8'0973—dc22   2004060556

Printed in the United States of America

CONTENTS

colonies' relationship to Great Britain to the relationship between slaves and their masters.

tion argues that the goal of the Civil War must be emancipation for all American slaves.

Chapter 5 • FROM EMANCIPATION TO CIVIL RIGHTS

FOREWORD

Historians Gary T. Marx and Douglas McAdam define a social movement as "organized efforts to promote or resist change in society that rely, at least in part, on noninstitutionalized forms of political action." Examining American social movements broadens and vitalizes the study of history by allowing students to observe the efforts of ordinary individuals and groups to oppose the established values of their era, often in unconventional ways. The civil rights movement of the twentieth century, for example, began as an effort to challenge legalized racial segregation and garner social and political rights for African Americans. Several grassroots organizations—groups of ordinary citizens committed to social activism—came together to organize boycotts, sit-ins, voter registration drives, and demonstrations to counteract racial discrimination. Initially, the movement faced massive opposition from white citizens, who had long been accustomed to the social standards that required the separation of the races in almost all areas of life. But the movement's consistent use of an innovative form of protest—nonviolent direct action—eventually aroused the public conscience, which in turn paved the way for major legislative victories such as the Civil Rights Act of 1964 and the Voting Rights Act of 1965. Examining the civil rights movement reveals how ordinary people can use nonstandard political strategies to change society.

Investigating the style, tactics, personalities, and ideologies of American social movements also encourages students to learn about aspects of history and culture that may receive scant attention in textbooks. As scholar Eric Foner notes, American history "has been constructed not only in congressional debates and political treatises, but also on plantations and picket lines, in parlors and bedrooms. Frederick Douglass, Eugene V. Debs, and Margaret Sanger . . . are its architects as well as Thomas Jefferson and Abraham Lincoln." While not all

American social movements garner popular support or lead to epoch-changing legislation, they each offer their own unique insight into a young democracy's political dialogue.

Each book in Greenhaven's American Social Movements series allows readers to follow the general progression of a particular social movement—examining its historical roots and beginnings in earlier chapters and relatively recent and contemporary information (or even the movement's demise) in later chapters. With the incorporation of both primary and secondary sources, as well as writings by both supporters and critics of the movement, each anthology provides an engaging panoramic view of its subject. Selections include a variety of readings, such as book excerpts, newspaper articles, speeches, manifestos, literary essays, interviews, and personal narratives. The editors of each volume aim to include the voices of movement leaders and participants as well as the opinions of historians, social analysts, and individuals who have been affected by the movement. This comprehensive approach gives students the opportunity to view these movements both as participants have experienced them and as historians and critics have interpreted them.

Every volume in the American Social Movements series includes an introductory essay that presents a broad historical overview of the movement in question. The annotated table of contents and comprehensive index help readers quickly locate material of interest. Each selection is preceded by an introductory paragraph that summarizes the article's content and provides historical context when necessary. Several other research aids are also present, including brief excerpts of supplementary material, a chronology of major events pertaining to the movement, and an accessible bibliography.

The Greenhaven Press American Social Movements series offers readers an informative introduction to some of the most fascinating groups and ideas in American history. The contents of each anthology provide a valuable resource for general readers as well as for enthusiasts of American political science, history, and culture.

Free at Last!

In 1619 a ship containing about a score of black Africans taken from their homeland by Dutch traders arrived at the British settlement in Jamestown, Virginia. The Africans were sold as slaves and pressed into service in Jamestown as farmworkers. These individuals were the first of a steady stream of Africans brought to North America against their will during the seventeenth century. Eventually slavery took root in every British colony in North America. The constitutions, charters, and legal codes of several of Great Britain's American colonies specifically permitted slavery or contained laws that governed the lives of slaves. After 1700 a brisk and profitable slave trade developed between Africa and North America. Africans were kidnapped or purchased on the west coast of Africa and shipped across the Atlantic Ocean to North America, where they were sold or traded for sugar, molasses, rum, and other American products.

Perhaps some residents of Jamestown, Virginia, raised their voices in protest when the first slaves arrived in that settlement in 1619. Many of the Quakers who settled in Pennsylvania during the seventeenth century opposed slavery on moral and religious grounds, and antislavery voices were heard in Puritan New England during the same time period. The oldest surviving antislavery text—*The Selling of Joseph*, published in 1700—was authored by a Puritan magistrate. A major slave uprising occurred in South Carolina in 1739, and the first abolitionist society in America formed in Philadelphia in 1775. When the American colonies declared their independence from Great Britain and formed themselves into a democratic republic, many Americans emphasized the contradiction between democracy and the institution of slavery.

But no vocal and organized abolitionist movement formed on American soil until the 1830s. When that movement finally formed, however, it quickly gathered momentum, divided the United States into proslavery and antislavery factions, and in 1861 propelled the nation into a great civil war that ultimately uprooted slavery from United States soil. After the passage of the Thirteenth Amendment to the U.S. Constitution, enacted in 1865, the forces that had galvanized to abolish slavery pressed for full citizenship rights for the freed slaves and their descendents. The abolitionist movement transitioned into a civil rights movement that continued into the twentieth century.

EARLY ABOLITIONIST VOICES

The first American abolitionists were individual, isolated voices disconnected from any organized colony-wide movement. No antislavery society formed before 1775, and no abolitionist newspaper circulated during the colonial era. As historian Dwight Lowell Dumond states, the colonial American "who opposed slavery did so, not because he had read a book, or newspaper, or otherwise digested an argument, but because he instinctively rejected a system of human relationships so utterly foreign to common decency."[1]

The oldest surviving American abolitionist text, *The Selling of Joseph*, appeared in 1700. Its author, Samuel Sewall, was a judge in Puritan Massachusetts Bay Colony. He articulated his opposition to slavery in a written communication to a fellow judge, John Saffin, who had ruled that a black indentured servant could not be freed even when his period of indentureship expired. Sewall argued that slavery was immoral because "all Men, as they are Sons of *Adam*, are Coheirs; and have equal Right unto Liberty, and all their outward Comforts of Life." Sewall used the biblical figure Joseph, whose brothers sold him into slavery in Egypt, as a basis for his opposition to slavery: *"Joseph* was rightfully no more a Slave to his Brethren, than they were to him; and they had no more Authority to *Sell* him than they had to *Slay* him."[2] Sewall's response to Judge Saffin was printed as a pamphlet titled *The Selling of Joseph* and distributed throughout Massachusetts.

Quakers who settled in Pennsylvania during the late seventeenth century were the first indentifiable colonial group to oppose slavery. According to historian Merton L. Dillon, "Quakers alone among religious groups in pre-Revolutionary America developed an ethic that demanded antislavery action."[3] Two eighteenth-century Quaker leaders, John Woolman and Anthony Benezet, wrote and worked passionately for the abolition of slavery. Woolman's pamphlet *Some Considerations on the Keeping of Negroes*, published in 1754, was more widely distributed than *The Selling of Joseph*. Benezet also penned antislavery pamphlets during the decade before the American Revolution.

SLAVERY AND THE AMERICAN REVOLUTION

By the time of the American Revolution, a growing number of Americans were beginning to believe that slavery violated natural law. In the Declaration of Independence, issued in 1776 by the Continental Congress, Thomas Jefferson, a Virginian who owned slaves, articulated the fundamental principles of natural law—"that all men are created equal, that they are endowed by their Creator with certain unalienable Rights, that among these are Life, Liberty, and the pursuit of Happiness." Jefferson's original draft of the Declaration included the charge against King George III of England that he had "waged cruel war against human nature itself, violating its most sacred right of life and liberty in the persons of a distant people who never offended him, captivating them into slavery in another hemisphere, or to incur miserable death in their transport thither."[4] But southern delegates to the Continental Congress opposed the inclusion of Jefferson's indictment against King George, and that passage concerning slavery was deleted from the document issued on July 4, 1776.

During and after the American Revolution, however, many Americans began to sense a contradiction between the noble sentiments about liberty articulated in the Declaration of Independence and the institution of slavery. Historian Merton L. Dillon states that "opponents of slavery during the Revolutionary era understandably viewed themselves as forming part of a great army of Americans whose activities in behalf of liberty were combining to usher in a more enlightened age."[5] Benjamin Franklin, John Adams, and other leaders of the American Revolution condemned slavery. Legislatures in the South passed laws allowing for the emancipation of slaves by individual owners, and legislatures in the North passed immediate or gradual emancipation laws. For example, in 1780 Massachusetts adopted a new constitution that outlawed slavery in that state.

But slavery survived the American Revolution and became a part of the new American republic that formed with the implementation of the U.S. Constitution in 1789. Although the words "slave" or "slavery" appeared nowhere in the original Constitution, the document offered protection for slave owners by recognizing slaves as property and guaranteeing that slaves who escaped to slave-free states would be legally returned to their owners.

SLAVERY IS ABOLISHED IN THE NORTH

Slavery began to disappear from the North during the last quarter of the eighteenth century. By that time a diverse economy was developing in the North. Although most northerners still lived on farms, an urban economy was maturing in Boston, New York, Philadelphia, and other northern cities—an economy driven by craftsmen and merchants rather than by farmers. By the end of the eighteenth century the Industrial Revolution, which had its birth in Great Britain, had traversed the Atlantic Ocean, resulting in the construction of mills in the North and the production of manufactured products.

Slavery was most conducive to an agricultural economy. With little training, slaves could be taught to plant, tend, and harvest crops and perform other farm tasks such as caring for livestock, clearing land, and constructing fences. Slavery was most profitable in a warm climate where farmhands worked almost year-round. The North's diverse economy and short growing season made slavery too costly. A northern farmer would have to house, feed, and clothe slaves for the whole year, but those slaves would work the land for only a few months. It

was more cost-effective for northern farmers to hire day laborers during the growing and harvest seasons than to maintain
slaves for the entire year. Training slaves as craftsmen or mill
workers was also prohibitively expensive. Hence, for economic
reasons slavery failed to become an important component of
the North's economy. Moreover, moral opposition to slavery by
religious groups such as the Quakers was more widespread in
the North than in the South. In 1794 the first national abolitionist society, the American Convention for Promoting the
Abolition of Slavery and Improving the Condition of the
African Race, formed in Philadelphia.

By 1804 all northern states had passed abolition legislation.
Some states enacted immediate emancipation laws, while others passed legislation that would abolish slavery gradually. For
example, in 1799 the New York legislature passed a law requiring that all New Yorkers born after July 4 of that year must be
set free at age twenty-eight (for men) or twenty-five (for
women). Thus, New York would be virtually slave free by 1827.

SLAVERY IN THE SOUTH

But slavery remained deeply rooted in the South's economy and
culture. In 1793 Eli Whitney, a New Englander, invented the
cotton gin, an inexpensive, easily copied machine that separated
seed from cotton fiber, significantly reducing the cost of pro-
cessing cotton. The South's soil, its long growing season, and the
new, more efficient "ginning" process made cotton the region's
"king crop." Textile mills in the North and in England readily
purchased southern cotton, which was planted, picked, and
processed by slave labor. For southern farmers, cotton became
an instant cash crop. A landowner could purchase land fairly
cheaply, acquire slaves to plant and harvest his cotton crop, sell
the cotton at a handsome profit, then use the profits to acquire
more land. In the South, a plantation society of wealthy
landowners developed into a cultural and economic aristocracy
captured a century later in Margaret Mitchell's best-selling
novel, *Gone with the Wind.*

Southern plantation owners and lawmakers resisted the abolitionist impulses coming from the North. Slavery had become vital to the South's economy. The institution was ardently defended in newspaper editorials, in legislative halls, and even from the pulpit. Southern ministers argued that slavery's presence in America allowed heathen Africans the opportunity to become aware of the Christian God, and that the Almighty had ordained that the proper relationship between the white and black races was master to slave.

THE ERA OF GOOD FEELING

For the first two decades of the nineteenth century, the North and South abided by an unwritten agreement regarding slavery. The South would not attempt to introduce the institution in the North, and the North would not interfere with slavery in the South. This unwritten agreement resulted in what has become known as the Era of Good Feeling. The new nation prospered as settlers moved westward into territory acquired by the Louisiana Purchase of 1803. In 1812 the United States defended itself in a war against Great Britain. The fledgling republican government outlined in the U.S. Constitution survived; its democratic institutions—Congress, the court system, the presidency—worked. In 1807 Congress, with few dissenting voices, passed the nation's first piece of abolitionist legislation—a bill that outlawed the importation of slaves from abroad.

But westward expansion tested the nation's slavery pact. As pioneers crossed the Mississippi River and settled the western frontier, the slavery issue moved to the top of the nation's political agenda. Would slavery be legal in the new U.S. territories west of the Mississippi River? When these territories entered the Union as states, would the new states be slave states or free states? Southern territories that entered the Union—Kentucky, Tennessee, Louisiana, Mississippi, Alabama—had become slave states because slavery had already taken root in those territories at the time of their admission to the Union. States carved from northern territories—Vermont, Ohio, Indiana, Illinois—had become free states. But the question of whether slavery would be permitted in the vast western territories was unresolved. As the

Civil War–era historian James M. McPherson states, "The slavery issue would probably have caused a showdown between North and South in any circumstances. But it was the country's sprawling growth that made the issue so explosive. Was the manifest destiny of those two million square miles west of the Mississippi River to be free or slave?"[6]

THE MISSOURI QUESTION

Missouri became a test for the nation's fragile agreement on slavery. In 1819 the Missouri Territory applied for statehood. Missouri shared its eastern border with Illinois, a free state, and Kentucky, a slave state. When Congress considered Missouri's admission to the Union, the slavery question was open for debate.

When Missouri applied for statehood, the nation comprised eleven free states and eleven slave states, a balance that protected the national truce over the slavery question. Most of the free territories slated for statehood were in the North, so southerners did not want Missouri to enter the Union as a free state and upset

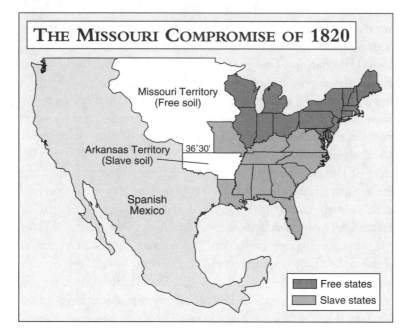

THE MISSOURI COMPROMISE OF 1820

Missouri Territory
(Free soil)

Arkansas Territory   36°30'
(Slave soil)

Spanish
Mexico

Free states
Slave states

the balance between free and slave states in Congress. But Representative James Tallmadge of New York introduced an antislavery amendment to the bill that would admit Missouri to the Union. The Tallmadge Amendment stated that no slaves could be legally imported into Missouri and that slaves already residing there would be freed when they reached the age of twenty-five. Tallmadge's amendment passed in the House of Representatives, where the northern states held a majority, but it was blocked by southern lawmakers in the Senate. The debate on the amendment was bitter in both legislative houses, and newspapers brought the congressional dispute into homes around the nation.

To resolve the Missouri question, Senator J.B. Thomas of Illinois proposed a compromise. Maine, a territory belonging to Massachusetts, would enter the Union as a free state, and Missouri would enter as a slave state. In addition, slavery would be made illegal in any territories acquired in the Louisiana Purchase north of latitude 36°30' north. This measure was designed to settle the question of slavery in the United States territories and prevent the kind of bitter congressional debate that accompanied Missouri's application for statehood.

Thomas's Missouri Compromise passed both houses of Congress and was signed into law by President James Monroe in 1820. But once raised in national debate, the slavery question would not soon fade from American politics. Thomas Jefferson, retired from politics and living at Monticello, his Virginia estate, worried that the geographical line drawn between free and slave territories would result in the division of his nation. Writing to a friend, John Holmes, in 1820, Jefferson asserted, "A geographical line, coinciding with a marked principle, moral and political, once conceived and held up to the angry passions of men, will never be obliterated; and every new irritation will mark it deeper and deeper."[7]

INCREASED TENSIONS OVER SLAVERY

Jefferson was correct. The Missouri debate galvanized isolated antislavery groups and raised antislavery voices in Congress, in the press, and from the pulpit. In 1821 the American Convention for Promoting the Abolition of Slavery and Improving the Condition of the African Race shifted its emphasis from improving the lives of slaves to advocating general emancipation. That same year Denmark Vesey, a former South Carolina slave who had won a lottery and purchased his freedom, began plotting a slave rebellion. He recruited slaves living in and around Charleston for his endeavor, but in 1822 Vesey was betrayed, foiling his plan. He and thirty-five of his accomplices were apprehended and later executed. The next year antislavery Illinoisans united to scuttle an amendment to their state's constitution that would legalize slavery.

Despite Vesey's failure other African American freemen began to work toward emancipation. In 1827 John Russworm, a New York freeman, founded *Freedom's Journal*, the first abolitionist newspaper published by African Americans. In 1829, David Walker, a Boston freeman, published *An Appeal to the Coloured Citizens of the World*, arguably the most militant antislavery text published before 1830. Walker's *Appeal*, which was widely distributed, delivered a ringing condemnation of American slavery. Walker depicted slave owners as sinners whose offense would one day be punished by a just and vengeful God: "There are not a more wretched, ignorant, miserable and abject set of beings in the world than the blacks in the southern and western sections of this country, under tyrants and devils.... O Americans! Americans! I call God—I call angels—I call men, to witness, that your *destruction* is at hand, and will be speedily consummated unless you *repent*."[8]

The South's response to abolitionist rhetoric from the North was predictable. Southerners defended their institution more vehemently, condemning abolitionists as radicals bent on destroying the Union. The Missouri Compromise of 1820, designed to resolve the slavery question, had actually widened the rift between North and South.

A NEW ABOLITIONIST NEWSPAPER

William Lloyd Garrison, a Massachusetts abolitionist, was swept up in the outpouring of antislavery sentiment that followed in the wake of the Missouri debates. In 1829, the year that Walker published his *Appeal*, Garrison was living in Baltimore and working on an abolitionist newspaper titled *Genius of Universal Emancipation*. Inspired by Walker's earnestness and eloquence, Garrison filled *Genius* with fiery editorials condemning slavery and calling for equal rights for all black Americans. Early in 1830 Garrison and Benjamin Lundy, the managing editor of *Genius*, were indicted by a Baltimore grand jury for libel because of an article that criticized a slave trader named Francis Todd. Garrison and Lundy were found guilty, and Garrison received a six-month jail sentence, imposed because he could not pay the fine of fifty dollars and court fees. After Garrison had spent forty-nine days in a Baltimore jail, a sympathizer paid the fine, and Garrison was released.

While Garrison and Lundy were being prosecuted, *Genius* failed, but Garrison's career as a newspaperman was not finished. Resolute in his desire to spread the antislavery gospel, and determined to show that the courts could not silence him, Garrison returned to Boston with plans to launch another antislavery newspaper. On January 1, 1831, he published the first issue of the *Liberator*. The paper was an unqualified success. It would appear weekly, without interruption, for the next thirty-five years and would shape the course of the slavery debate in the United States. According to Henry Mayer, a Garrison biographer, the *Liberator* "made the public listen in a way that [Garrison's] predecessors had not . . . and [Garrison] made the moral issue of slavery so palpable that it could no longer be evaded."[9]

An editorial in the opening issue of the *Liberator* boldly announced Garrison's mission: "I shall strenuously contend for the immediate enfranchisement of our slave population. . . . I am in earnest—I will not equivocate—I will not excuse—I will not retreat a single inch AND I WILL BE HEARD."[10] According to Mayer, Garrison, in the *Liberator*, "employed a writing style of extraordinary physicality—in his columns trumpets blare, statues bleed, hearts melt, apologists tremble, light blazes, nations move."[11] The newspaper spread Garrison's abolitionist gospel across the United States, making Garrison a national figure and uniting abolitionists into a national network. Garrison also formed alliances with abolitionist organizations in Great Britain, giving his movement an international thrust.

GARRISON AND NAT TURNER'S REBELLION

So immediately influential was Garrison's newspaper that he was blamed for a slave rebellion directed by a Southampton, Virginia, slave, Nat Turner, during the summer of 1831. According to his critics Garrison's abolitionist rhetoric had inspired Turner, a self-ordained slave preacher who claimed to have experienced visitations from God, to turn on his master and ignite a slave uprising that took the lives of sixty white people in and around Southampton. South Carolina and Georgia offered rewards for Garrison's arrest for libel, and Garrison received threatening letters from across the South. Abolitionists responded with letters of support and money for Garrison's newspaper.

Encouraged by support from around the United States, Garrison worked during the next two years to establish a national antislavery organization—an association that would unite all enemies of slavery in a common cause. In 1833 Garrison formed the American Anti-Slavery Society and served as its first president, while he continued to publish weekly editions of the *Liberator*. In the face of Garrison's more aggressive form of abolition, Southern slave owners defended their institution more forcefully. Sometimes fraying tensions between proslavery and antislavery Americans resulted in violence. In 1837, for example, two hundred proslavery individuals attacked the editorial offices of the *Observer*, an abolitionist newspaper published in Alton, Illinois, a town on the Mississippi River. The newspaper's editor, Reverend Elijah Lovejoy, fired a shot at the mob attacking his offices. One man fell dead, and the mob attacked and killed Lovejoy.

A NATIONAL MOVEMENT

By the mid-1830s Garrison's call for abolition had developed into a national movement. Abolitionist newspapers sprouted up across the nation. Abolitionist publishers poured out antislavery texts such as Theodore D. Weld's influential *American Slavery as*

It Is, published in 1839. Men of letters, such as the essayist Henry David Thoreau and the poet John Greenleaf Whittier, joined the movement, as did influential clergymen such as Lyman Beecher, Theodore Parker, and William Ellery Channing. During the 1830s abolitionists formed the Underground Railroad, a network of safe houses and hiding places where escaped slaves could conceal themselves as they traveled toward freedom in the northern states or Canada.

Women, too, enlisted in the antislavery crusade. The abolitionist movement was the first American political movement in which women played a major role. In the mid-nineteenth century, American women had no formal involvement in politics; they could neither vote nor run for political office. But antislavery women had a major impact on the abolitionist movement. In 1836 Angelina Grimké, who was born in South Carolina but who opposed slavery, authored a pamphlet titled *Appeal to the Christian Women of the South*. In that statement Grimké identifies four actions that women can take to signal their opposition to slavery: "1st. You can read on this subject. 2d. You can pray over this subject. 3d. You can speak on this subject. 4th. You can *act* on this subject."[12] Lydia Maria Child, the author of an 1833 pamphlet titled *An Appeal in Favor of That Class of Americans Called Africans*, became the editor in 1841 of the *National Anti-Slavery Standard*, an abolitionist newspaper published in New York. One of the most effective conductors on the Underground Railroad was a woman—Harriet Tubman, who personally helped hundreds of slaves escape from bondage.

The most effective piece of abolitionist writing was authored by a woman. In 1851 Harriet Beecher Stowe, the daughter of abolitionist clergyman Lyman Beecher, began publishing a series of sketches on a fictional slave named Uncle Tom in *National Era*, an abolitionist newspaper. Those sketches captivated the newspaper's antislavery readership. *National Era* carried Stowe's tale of Uncle Tom for more than a year, after which the sketches were published in 1852 as the moving novel *Uncle Tom's Cabin*. The book became an immediate national bestseller, smashing sales records and establishing Stowe as a noteworthy

American novelist and a major voice in the abolitionist movement. Capitalizing on her literary fame, Stowe became active on the abolitionist lecture circuit.

FREDERICK DOUGLASS JOINS THE MOVEMENT

The abolitionist movement was also the first American social movement in which African Americans played a vital role. During the late eighteenth century Olaudah Equiano, a freed slave, published an autobiography, *The Interesting Narrative of the Life of Olaudah Equiano, or Gustavus Vassa, the African, Written by Himself*, and became active in the movement to abolish the international slave trade. Other slave narratives appeared during the nineteenth century, as did Walker's *Appeal* and *The Confessions of Nat Turner*, the tale of Turner's 1831 uprising.

No African American had more influence on the direction of mid-nineteenth-century abolitionist politics, however, than Frederick Douglass. Douglass, who escaped from slavery in Maryland as a young man, met Garrison in Massachusetts and enlisted in Garrison's antislavery movement. A self-taught reader and writer and a fiery and eloquent orator, Douglass joined Garrison on the abolitionist lecture circuit and contributed articles to the *Liberator*. In 1845 Douglass published the first of three autobiographies, *Narrative of the Life of Frederick Douglass, an American Slave*. The book, which details Douglass's life as a slave and the dehumanizing conditions of the lives of slaves, became an immediate publishing success. Encouraged by the popularity of his narrative, in 1847 Douglass established his own newspaper, *North Star*, which advocated immediate emancipation and full citizenship rights for African Americans and American women. By 1850 Douglass, an ex-slave, had become the most famous African American.

THE SLAVERY DEBATE DIVIDES THE NATION

By the 1840s the slavery question had found its way into every important national political debate. When war broke out between the United States and Mexico in 1846, abolitionists charged that the conflict was being waged mainly to acquire additional slave territory. At the start of the war Representative David Wilmot of Pennsylvania introduced in Congress the Wilmot Proviso, a bill that would make slavery illegal in any newly acquired U.S. territory. The bill never passed, but the long and bitter debate over the Wilmot Proviso further divided proslavery and antislavery voices in Congress.

In 1849 the slavery debate flared again when the California territory applied for statehood. Southerners opposed California's application because it would add a free state to the Union. To appease southern lawmakers, Senators Henry Clay of Kentucky and Stephen Douglas of Illinois crafted what became known as the Compromise of 1850. The Clay-Douglas bill contained four main elements: California would enter the Union as a free state; New Mexico and Utah would be established as separate territories with the question of slavery to be settled in the future by the local populations; the buying and selling of slaves would be made illegal in Washington, D.C.; and a new Fugitive Slave Law would better enable southern slave owners to recover escaped slaves.

The compromise bill passed and became law, but abolitionists vigorously opposed it, particularly the Fugitive Slave Law, which mandated the appointment of federal commissioners in each state to help apprehend runaway slaves. These commissioners could form posses to track down escaped slaves and would be paid a bounty for each captured runaway. An African American accused of being a refugee slave would not have the right to a jury trial or an attorney and could not even present testimony on his own behalf. As a result, many freemen were apprehended as runaway slaves and pressed into slavery. Thoreau, already active on the abolitionist lecture circuit, stated that the Fugitive Slave Law "rises not to the level of the head; its natural habitat is the dirt. It was born and bred, and has its life only in the dust and mire . . . so trample it under foot."[13]

The Compromise of 1850 failed to end the animosity that had developed between the North and the South. Abolitionists had moved from the nation's political fringe into the mainstream and now began to challenge any southern political initiative that touched on the slavery question. In 1854 Congress's efforts to organize the Kansas-Nebraska territories initiated another crisis over slavery.

In organizing the Kansas-Nebraska territories, congressmen again had to resolve the slavery question. These territories lay north of latitude 36°30' north, but Senator Douglas, sidestepping the Missouri Compromise that outlawed slavery in U.S. territories north of that mark, proposed that the local populations determine the question of slavery in Kansas and Nebraska. Douglas referred to this concept as popular sovereignty. He shepherded his Kansas-Nebraska bill through Congress, and it was signed into law by President Franklin Pierce in May 1854.

Again, abolitionists were outraged. The antislavery press crucified Douglas for forging a partnership with the slaveholders. Antislavery northerners began speaking of a Slave Power, consisting of southern plantation owners and the congressmen who represented them, whose goal was to make slavery legal in every state and U.S. territory. Garrison called the Kansas-Nebraska Act "diabolical"[14] and led protests against the new law on July 4, 1854.

As the date for Kansas's entry into the Union neared, slaveholders and antislavery northerners streamed into the territory. Inevitably the two forces clashed, and civil war broke out. By 1856 Kansas was known as "Bleeding Kansas," and federal troops were eventually sent to the territory to restore peace.

THE EMERGENCE OF LINCOLN AND THE REPUBLICAN PARTY

After passage of the Kansas-Nebraska Act, the Whig Party, Liberty Party, and Free-Soil Party, which included many antislavery northerners, splintered, weakened, or disintegrated. Antislavery northerners began holding conventions in the North and Midwest for the purpose of forming a new antislavery party. By 1856 the Republican Party had formed. Its mission was to cur-

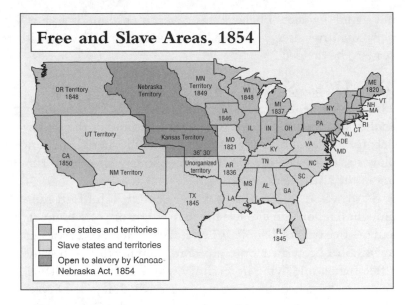

Free and Slave Areas, 1854

OR Territory 1848

Nebraska Territory

MN Territory 1849

WI 1848

MI 1837

ME 1820

NH
VT
MA

NY

UT Territory

Kansas Territory

IA 1846

IL

IN

OH

PA

RI
CT
NJ
DE
MD

CA 1850

NM Territory

36° 30'

Unorganized territory

MO 1821

KY

VA

AR 1836

TN

NC

SC

MS

AL

GA

TX 1845

LA

FL 1845

Free states and territories

Slave states and territories

Open to slavery by Kansas-Nebraska Act, 1854

tail the spread of slavery in the United States. In the 1856 presidential election, the Republican Party's candidate, John Frémont, carried eleven states.

One former Whig who joined the new party was Abraham Lincoln of Illinois. A former Illinois congressman, Lincoln had virtually retired from politics after his term in Congress ended in 1849. The passage of the Kansas–Nebraska Act, however, outraged Lincoln and brought him back into the political fray. In a speech in Peoria, Illinois, in October 1854, Lincoln asserted, "This *declared* indifference, but as I must think, covert *real zeal* for the spread of slavery, I can not but hate. I hate it because of the monstrous injustice of slavery itself."[15] Within a few years Lincoln would become a nationally known figure in the Republican Party. In 1858, he challenged Douglas for his Illinois Senate seat. Lincoln lost, but his debates with Douglas on slavery and popular sovereignty were printed in newspapers across the United States, making all antislavery Americans familiar with Abe Lincoln of Illinois. Lincoln had kicked off his Senate campaign with a speech that became known as his "House Divided" speech. "A house divided against itself cannot stand," he said. "I believe this government cannot endure, permanently half *slave* and half *free*—but I *do* believe it will cease to be divided."[16]

THE *DRED SCOTT* CASE

The passage of the Kansas-Nebraska Act suggested to many abolitionists that the South was gaining ground in the slavery debate. The abolitionist movement took another significant blow in 1857 when the U.S. Supreme Court delivered its ruling in the *Dred Scott* case.

Scott was a Missouri slave whose master, John Emerson, brought him for a time to live in the free territory of Minnesota and the free state of Illinois. When Emerson and Scott returned to Missouri, Scott sued for his freedom, claiming that he became a free man while living in territory where slavery was illegal. Scott's case reached the Supreme Court, which rejected Scott's claim. Chief Justice Roger Taney, delivering the Court's opinion, asserted that Scott, as a slave, was a piece of property, and that his owner retained possession of him as he traveled through free territory, just as his owner would retain possession of his horse and wagon as he traveled from state to state. Moreover, the Court ruled that even if Emerson remained in a free state indefinitely, he would continue to own Scott.

The ruling outraged abolitionists. If one slave owner could retain one slave when he moved into free territory, why could not an owner move ten or a hundred slaves into free territory and retain possession of them? Lincoln quickly sensed the danger of the *Dred Scott* decision. He predicted a *Dred Scott II* ruling that would negate the antislavery clauses of the free-state constitutions—and then slavery would be legal everywhere in the United States.

Although the crises of the 1850s united abolitionists across the North in a common purpose, fault lines developed within the movement. The Christian abolitionists, whose opposition to slavery was religiously based, maintained that prayer and moral suasion, not political activism, were the most potent weapons to use in the abolitionist cause. Members of the Republican Party disagreed, arguing that slavery was a political as well as a moral problem that could be dealt with within the existing political system.

More radical factions also emerged within the movement. By the 1850s Garrison was calling for the North's secession from the Union. If the North seceded, Garrison argued, it could establish itself as a slave-free nation that would provide political asylum for runaway slaves. "No Union with slaveholders" became Garrison's motto. Garrison embraced pacifism, but some elements within the abolitionist movement advocated Nat Turner–style uprisings to rid America of slavery.

JOHN BROWN'S RAID

John Brown, an Ohio-born abolitionist, sensed that prayer, moral suasion, and political maneuvering would not check the advances that the Slave Power had made during the 1850s. Brown had participated in the civil war in "Bleeding Kansas," and he was not opposed to using force to achieve his goals. After he had heard of the Supreme Court's resolution of the *Dred Scott* case, Brown committed himself to strike a serious blow at the Slave Power. He developed a plan to capture the federal arms arsenal in Harpers Ferry, Virginia, arm the slaves living on nearby plantations, and ignite a slave revolt that would spread across Virginia and to its neighboring states.

On October 16, 1859, Brown and his twenty-one followers moved on Harpers Ferry, surprising sentries guarding the town and arms arsenal. A night watchman was killed by one of Brown's men. For several hours Brown and his comrades controlled Harpers Ferry and its munitions warehouses. By the next morning, however, word had reached President James Buchanan that federal buildings were under attack. The president sent marines, under the command of Colonel Robert E. Lee, to take back the town and federal arsenal. Brown and his men were quickly surrounded by Lee's troops. After brief negotiations failed, a skirmish ensued, during which several of Brown's comrades were killed. Brown was wounded and taken captive. Brown's slave revolt lasted only thirty-six hours and freed not a single slave. Brown was tried and found guilty of murder and treason. He was hanged in December.

Although Brown's raid had been a total failure, it energized abolitionists and prompted great outrage in the South. At the hour of Brown's execution church bells rang throughout the North, and abolitionists prayed for a martyr. Thoreau offered an address in Massachusetts titled "A Plea for Captain John Brown"; he praised Brown as a man who moved "against the legions of Slavery, in obedience to an infinitely higher command."[17] In the South, however, Brown was condemned as a satanic traitor who tried to ignite a civil war. Southerners blamed the abolitionists and the Republicans for encouraging and supporting Brown's raid.

The era of compromise between North and South was over. In Washington, D.C., lawmakers came to the Senate and House of Representatives armed. During one heated debate in the House over the Brown affair, Representative William Barksdale of Mississippi attacked with a knife Representative Thaddeus Stevens of Pennsylvania, an abolitionist. Neither man was seriously injured because colleagues acted promptly to separate the two men, but the incident foreshadowed an armed conflict between the North and the South over slavery.

THE ELECTION OF 1860

The presidential election of 1860 provided the spark that started the conflict. The Republicans nominated Lincoln as their presidential candidate. His election platform called for no further expansion of slavery in the United States. The Democrats, bitterly divided over the slavery question, could not settle on a single candidate. Northern Democrats nominated Douglas, and southern Democrats nominated Vice President John Breckinridge. A third party, the Constitutional Union Party, nominated John Bell as its presidential candidate. With his opposition hopelessly divided, Lincoln won the election even though he carried not one southern state.

The South's reaction was predictable. Fearing that an abolitionist had won the White House, seven southern states voted to secede from the Union even before Lincoln took office. In his inaugural address, delivered on March 4, 1861, Lincoln pledged not to interfere with slavery in the states in which it already existed, but he could not placate the rebellious southern states. He began his term in office as the president of a nation divided over slavery.

THE CIVIL WAR

In April 1861 the cold war between the North and the rebellious southern states turned into a violent civil war when the South Carolina militia attacked Fort Sumter, a federal garrison in Charleston Harbor. Fort Sumter fell, and Lincoln called for volunteers to enlist in the Union army and put down the rebellion. Four additional states joined the rebellion, forming the eleven-state Confederate States of America. In July, a federal army of thirty-five thousand men marched from Washington, D.C., toward Richmond, the capital of the confederacy. The Union army was badly beaten in the Battle of Bull Run, signaling that the rebellion would not be easily suppressed.

Initially, Lincoln viewed the conflict between the North and the South as a war to quell a rebellion, not a confrontation over slavery. He informed the Confederate States that they could return to the Union with slavery in place. As the conflict dragged on, however, abolitionists within Lincoln's party urged him to issue an emancipation decree. "The present policy of our Government is evidently to put down the slaveholding rebellion, and at the same time protect and preserve slavery. This policy hangs like a millstone about the neck of our people,"[18] wrote Douglass in his newspaper. Gradually Lincoln realized that the rift between the North and the South could not be bridged unless the slavery question was permanently settled. First, he urged the slave states to pass laws to abolish slavery gradually over a period of years, and in return the federal government would compensate slave owners for each slave freed. When no slave states considered his offer, Lincoln made plans to issue a general emancipation decree.

The Emancipation Proclamation

During the summer of 1862 Lincoln drafted an emancipation proclamation that he shared only with the members of his cabinet. His advisers counseled Lincoln to withhold issuance of the decree until the Union army won an important battlefield victory. On September 22, 1862, five days after the Union army stopped a Confederate advance at the Battle of Antietam in Sharpsburg, Maryland, Lincoln issued the Preliminary Emancipation Proclamation. The proclamation stated that all slaves in the rebellious states would be declared free on January 1, 1863, unless those states ended their rebellion and reentered the Union. No southern state accepted Lincoln's offer, so on January 1, 1863, Lincoln ordered the Emancipation Proclamation.

Lincoln's proclamation was greeted with celebrations throughout the North. Freed slaves saw January 1, 1863, as a day of jubilee. Abolitionist newspapers praised the president's decision in joyful editorials. But the Emancipation Proclamation would be meaningless if the North did not win the war; the North would have to defeat the South on the battlefield and force emancipation upon it. During the summer of 1863 the tide of the war changed as the North gained advantage after important victories at Gettysburg and Vicksburg.

The Thirteenth Amendment

Lincoln had some doubts about the legality of his Emancipation Proclamation, so he worked to give it the force of a constitutional amendment. Early in 1864 the Congress, with Lincoln's approval, began discussing a Thirteenth Amendment to the Constitution that would permanently outlaw slavery in all states and U.S. territories. The process of ratifying the Thirteenth Amendment would require a two-thirds approval vote in both the House of Representatives and the Senate and ratification by three-fourths of the individual state legislatures. In April 1864 the Senate approved the amendment, but approval in the House did not occur until January 31, 1865. By that time the North had attained the upper hand in the war, so complete emancipation was imminent.

One by one, individual state legislatures ratified the Thirteenth Amendment—a process that took until December 18, 1865. By that time Lincoln was dead—the victim of an assassin's bullet in April 1865—and the Civil War was over. The key section of the Thirteenth Amendment reads as follows: "Neither slavery nor involuntary servitude, except as a punishment for crime whereof the party shall have been duly convicted, shall exist within the United Sates, or any place subject to their jurisdiction."

The abolitionist movement had succeeded; American slaves were forever free, and slavery as an American institution was dead. "My vocation as an Abolitionist, thank God, is ended,"[19] exclaimed Garrison. He closed the *Liberator*, its mission having been completed.

CIVIL RIGHTS FOR THE FREEDMEN

In the aftermath of the Civil War, an era called Reconstruction, abolitionists, their immediate goal having been achieved, united to advocate full citizenship rights for African Americans. Douglass, fellow abolitionist Wendell Phillips, and leading congressional Republicans proposed civil rights legislation and two constitutional amendments to secure the citizenship rights of the freed slaves and their descendents. The Fourteenth Amendment, ratified in 1868, made all persons born in the United States and its territories citizens and guaranteed all citizens "equal protections of the laws." The Fifteenth Amendment, enacted in 1870, extended voting rights to African American men.

Despite the passage of these two constitutional amendments, securing full citizenship rights for African Americans turned into a long and difficult struggle. As the historian Robert W. Johannsen stated, "Reconstruction, like the Civil War, was a great tragedy," in part because "its social and humanitarian purposes . . . were soon discarded."[20] Ninety years after the conclusion of the Civil War, many African Americans still could not vote or run for political office; they could not attend public school with white students; they could not use public facilities such as libraries, beaches, and parks; and they could not patronize certain hotels, restaurants, theaters, or stadiums. During the 1950s, a century after the nation divided over slavery, a civil rights movement, the grandchild of the nineteenth-century abolitionist movement, swept the United States and effected changes in the American racial landscape as profound as those brought about by the abolitionist movement and the Civil War. In one of his great speeches, the leader of the civil rights movement of the mid-twentieth century, the Reverend Martin Luther King Jr., recalled his ancestors in bondage when he exclaimed, "Free at last, free at last, thank God Almighty, we are free at last."[21]

NOTES

1. Dwight Lowell Dumond, *Antislavery: The Crusade for Freedom in America.* New York: W.W. Norton, 1961, p. 16.

2. Quoted in Mason Lowance, ed., *Against Slavery: An Abolitionist Reader.* New York: Penguin, 2000, pp. 12–13.

3. Merton L. Dillon, *The Abolitionists: The Growth of a Dissenting Minority.* DeKalb: Northern Illinois University Press, 1974, p. 7.

4. Quoted in Philip S. Foner, ed., *The Basic Writings of Thomas Jefferson.* Garden City, NY: Halcyon, 1950, p. 7.

5. Dillon, *The Abolitionists*, p. 6.

6. James M. McPherson, *Battle Cry of Freedom: The Civil War Era.* New York: Oxford University Press, 1988, p. 8.

7. Quoted in Foner, *The Basic Writings of Thomas Jefferson*, p. 767.

8. Quoted in Diane Ravitch, ed., *The American Reader: Words That Moved a Nation.* New York: HarperCollins, 1990, p. 101.

9. Henry Mayer, *All on Fire: William Lloyd Garrison and the Abolition of Slavery.* New York: St. Martin's, 1998, p. 112.

10. Quoted in George M. Fredrickson, ed., *William Lloyd Garrison.* Englewood Cliffs, NJ: Prentice-Hall, 1968, p. 23.

11. Mayer, *All on Fire*, p. 112.

12. Quoted in Larry Ceplair, ed., *The Public Years of Sarah and Angelina Grimké: Selected Writings, 1835–1839.* New York: Columbia University Press, 1989, p. 55.

13. Henry David Thoreau, *"Civil Disobedience" and Other Essays.* New York: Dover, 1993, p. 23.

14. Quoted in Mayer, *All on Fire*, p. 440.

15. Abraham Lincoln, *Selected Speeches and Writings.* New York: Vintage, 1992, p. 94.

16. Lincoln, *Selected Speeches and Writings*, p. 131.

17. Thoreau, *"Civil Disobedience" and Other Essays*, p. 36.

18. Quoted in Richard A. Long, ed., *Black Writers and the American Civil War.* Secaucus, NJ: Blue and Grey Press, 1988, p. 273.

19. Quoted in Eric Foner, *Reconstruction: America's Unfinished Revolution, 1863–1877.* New York: Harper & Row, 1988, p. 67.

20. Robert W. Johannsen, ed., *Reconstruction, 1865–1877.* New York: Free Press, 1970, p. 21.

21. Quoted in James M. Washington, ed., *I Have a Dream: Writings and Speeches That Changed the World.* San Francisco: HarperSanFrancisco, 1992, p. 106.

CHAPTER 1

ABOLITIONIST VOICES IN COLONIAL AMERICA

AMERICAN
SOCIAL
MOVEMENTS

A Puritan Magistrate Condemns Slavery

SAMUEL SEWALL

In 1700, Samuel Sewall, a judge in Puritan Massachusetts Bay Colony, engaged a colleague on the bench, John Saffin, in a written debate on the morality of slavery. Saffin had ordered an African American indentured servant to remain in bondage even though the servant's period of indentureship had expired. Sewall criticized Saffin's ruling; and in doing so, he presented a religious critique of slavery as it was practiced in colonial Massachusetts. According to Sewall, slavery violated God's will because all human beings are sons of Adam who have "equal Right to Liberty, and all other outward Comforts of Life." Sewall's response to Saffin's ruling was published as a pamphlet titled *The Selling of Joseph*, the title coming from the biblical Joseph whose brothers sold him into slavery in Egypt. *The Selling of Joseph* is the oldest surviving American antislavery text.

F orasmuch *as* Liberty *is in real value next unto* Life: *None ought to part with it themselves, or deprive others of it, but upon most mature consideration.*

The Numerousness of Slaves at this Day in the Province, and the Uneasiness of them under their Slavery, hath put many upon thinking whether the Foundation of it be firmly and well laid; so as to sustain the Vast Weight that is built upon it. It is most certain that all Men, as they are the Sons of *Adam*, are Coheirs, and have equal Right unto Liberty, and all other outward Comforts of Life. God *hath given the Earth [with all its commodities] unto the Sons of Adam, Psal., 115, 16. And hath made of one Blood all Nations of Men, for to dwell on all the face of the Earth, and hath determined the Times before appointed, and the bounds of their*

Samuel Sewall, *The Selling of Joseph: A Memorial*. Boston: Bartholomew Green and John Allen, 1700.

Habitation: That they should seek the Lord. Forasmuch then as we are the Offspring of God, &c. *Acts* 17. 26, 27, 29. Now, although the Title given by the last Adam doth infinitely better Men's Estates, respecting God and themselves; and grants them a most beneficial and inviolable Lease under the Broad Seal of Heaven, who were before only Tenants at Will; yet through the Indulgence of God to our First Parents after the Fall, the outward Estate of all and every of their Children, remains the same as to one another. So that Originally, and Naturally, there is no such thing as Slavery. *Joseph* was rightfully no more a Slave to his Brethren, than they were to him; and they had no more Authority to *Sell* him, than they had to *Slay* him. And if *they* had nothing to do to sell him; the *Ishmaelites* bargaining with them, and paying down Twenty pieces of Silver, could not make a Title. Neither could *Potiphar* have any better Interest in him than the *Ishmaelites* had. *Gen.* 37, 20, 27, 28. For he that shall in this case plead *Alteration of Property*, seems to have forfeited a great part of his own claim to Humanity. There is no proportion between Twenty Pieces of Silver and Liberty. The Commodity itself is the Claimer. If *Arabian* Gold be imported in any quantities, most are afraid to meddle with it, though they might have it at easy rates; lest it should have been wrongfully taken from the Owners, it should kindle a fire to the Consumption of their whole Estate. 'Tis pity there should be more Caution used in buying a Horse, or a little lifeless dust, than there is in purchasing Men and Women: Whereas they are the Offspring of God, and their Liberty is,

. . . Auro pretiosior Omni [To Each More Precious than Gold].

And seeing God hath said, *He that Stealeth a Man, and Selleth him, or if he be found in his Hand, he shall surely be put to Death.* Exod. 21, 16. This Law being of Everlasting Equity, wherein Man-Stealing is ranked among the most atrocious of Capital Crimes: What louder Cry can there be made of that Celebrated Warning.

Caveat Emptor! [Buyer Beware!]

And all things considered, it would conduce more to the Welfare of the Province, to have White Servants for a Term of Years, than to have Slaves for Life. Few can endure to hear of a Negro's being made free; and indeed they can seldom use their Freedom well; yet their continual aspiring after their forbidden Liberty, renders them Unwilling Servants. And there is such a disparity in their Conditions, Colour, and Hair, that they can

A Response to
The Selling of Joseph

In 1701, John Saffin published a reply to Samuel Sewall's The Selling of Joseph. *In his reply, Saffin, a judge, argued that all human beings need not be treated as equals, as Sewall suggests.*

We grant it for a certain and undeniable verity, That all Mankind are the Sons and Daughters of *Adam*, and the Creatures of God. But it doth not therefore follow that we are bound to love and respect all men alike. . . . I may love my servant well, but my Son better; Charity begins at home, it would be a violation of common prudence, and a breach of good manners to treat a Prince like a Peasant. And this worthy Gentleman would deem himself much neglected, if we should show him no more Defference than to an ordinary Porter: And therefore these florid expressions, the Sons and Daughters of the First *Adam*, the Brethren and Sisters of the Second *Adam*, and the Offspring of God, seem to be misapplied to import and insinuate, that we ought to tender Pagan Negroes with all love and kindness, and equal respect as to the best of men.

William Dudley, ed., *Slavery: Opposing Viewpoints.* San Diego: Greenhaven Press, 1992, p. 35.

never embody with us, & grow up in orderly Families, to the Peopling of the Land; but still remain in our Body Politick as a kind of extravasat Blood. As many Negro Men as there are among us, so many empty Places are there in our Train Bands, and the places taken up of Men that might make Husbands for our Daughters. And the Sons and Daughters of *New England* would become more like *Jacob* and *Rachel*, if this Slavery were thrust quite out of Doors. Moreover it is too well known what Temptations Masters are under, to connive at the Fornication of their Slaves; lest they should be obliged to find them Wives, or pay their Fines. It seems to be practically pleaded that they might be lawless; 'tis thought much of, that the Law should have satisfaction for their Thefts, and other Immoralities; by which means, *Holiness to the Lord* is more rarely engraven upon this sort of Servitude. It is likewise most lamentable to think, how in taking Negroes out of *Africa*, and selling of them here, That which God has joined together, Men do boldly rend asunder; Men from their Country, Husbands from their Wives, Parents from their Children. How horrible is the Uncleanness, Mortality, if not Murder, that the Ships are guilty of that bring great Crouds of these miserable Men and Women. Me-thinks when we are bemoaning the barbarous Usage of our Friends and Kinsfolk in *Africa*, it might not be unreasonable to enquire whether we are not culpable in forcing the *Africans* to become Slaves amongst ourselves. And it may be a question whether all the Benefit received by *Negro* Slaves will balance the Accompt of Cash laid out upon them; and for the Redemption of our own enslaves Friends out of *Africa*. Besides all the Persons and Estates that have perished there.

OBJECTIONS AND ANSWERS

Obj. 1. *These Blackamores are of the Posterity of Cham, and therefore are under the Curse of Slavery.* Gen. 9, 25, 26, 27.

Ans. Of all Offices, one would not beg this; viz. Uncall'd for, to be an Executioner of the Vindictive Wrath of God; the extent and duration of which is to us uncertain. If this ever was a Commission; How do we know but it is long since out of

Date? Many have found it to their Cost, that a Prophetical Denunciation of Judgment against a Person or People, would not warrant them to inflict that evil. If it would, *Hazael* might justify himself in all he did against his master, and the *Israelites* from *2 Kings* 8, 10, 12.

But it is possible that by cursory reading, this Text may have been mistaken. For *Canaan* is the Person Cursed three times over, without the mentioning of *Cham*. Good Expositors suppose the Curse entailed on him, and that this Prophesie was accomplished in the Extirpation of the *Canaanites*, and in the Servitude of the *Gibeonites*. . . . Whereas the Blackamores are not descended of *Canaan*, but of *Cush*. Psal. 68, 31. *Princes shall come out of Egypt* [Mizraim]. *Ethiopia* [Cush] *shall soon stretch out her hands unto God.* Under which Names, all *Africa* may be comprehended; and their Promised Conversion ought to be prayed for. *Jer.* 13, 23. *Can the Ethiopian change his Skin?* This shows that Black Men are the Posterity of *Cush*. Who time out of mind have been distinguished by their Colour. . . .

Obj. 2. *The* Nigers *are brought out of a Pagan Country, into places where the Gospel is preached.*

Ans. Evil must not be done, that good may come of it. The extraordinary and comprehensive Benefit accruing to the Church of God, and to *Joseph* personally, did not rectify his Brethren's Sale of him.

Obj. 3. *The Africans have Wars one with another: Our Ships bring lawful Captives taken in those wars.*

Ans. For aught is known, their Wars are much such as were between *Jacob's* Sons and their Brother *Joseph.* If they be between Town and Town; Provincial or National: Every War is upon one side Unjust. An Unlawful War can't make lawful Captives. And by receiving, we are in danger to promote, and partake in their Barbarous Cruelties. I am sure, if some Gentlemen should go down to the *Brewsters* to take the Air, and Fish: And a stronger Party from *Hull* should surprise them, and sell them for Slaves to a Ship outward bound; they would think themselves unjustly dealt with; both by Sellers and Buyers. And yet 'tis to be feared, we have no other Kind of Title to our *Nigers. Therefore all things whatsoever ye would that men should do to you, do you even so to them: for this is the Law and the Prophets.* Matt. 7, 12.

Obj. 4. Abraham *had Servants bought with his Money and born in his House.*

Ans. Until the Circumstances of *Abraham's* purchase be recorded, no Argument can be drawn from it. In the mean time, Charity obliges us to conclude, that He knew it was lawful and good.

CHRISTIANS AND SLAVERY

It is Observable that the *Israelites* were strictly forbidden the buying or selling one another for Slaves. *Levit.* 25. 39. 46. *Jer.* 34. 8-22. And God gaged His Blessing in lieu of any loss they might conceit they suffered thereby, *Deut.* 15. 18. And since the partition Wall is broken down, inordinate Self-love should likewise be demolished. God expects that Christians should be of a more Ingenuous and benign frame of Spirit. Christians should carry it to all the World, as the *Israelites* were to carry it one towards another. And for Men obstinately to persist in holding their Neighbours and Brethren under the Rigor of perpetual Bondage, seems to be no proper way of gaining Assurance that God has given them Spiritual Freedom. Our Blessed Saviour has altered the Measures of the ancient Love Song, and set it to a most Excellent New Tune, which all ought to be ambitious of Learning. *Matt.* 5. 43. 44. *John* 13. 34. These *Ethiopians*, as black as they are, seeing they are the Sons and Daughters of the First *Adam*, the Brethren and Sisters of the Last Adam, and the Offspring of God; They ought to be treated with a Respect agreeable.

The Quaker Critique of American Slavery

DWIGHT LOWELL DUMOND

Dwight Lowell Dumond, an American historian who served on the faculty at the University of Michigan, is the author of three books on the slavery and Civil War eras. In this excerpt from *Antislavery: The Crusade for Freedom in America*, Dumond details abolitionist sentiment among the Pennsylvania Quakers during the mid-eighteenth century. The Quakers, who emphasized in their religious teachings the brotherhood of all human beings, considered slavery both a moral wrong and a sin, and they outlawed the practice in their religious communities. Dumond highlights the careers of two prominent eighteenth-century Quaker leaders, John Woolman and Anthony Benezet, both of whom wrote antislavery texts.

There were no antislavery societies and no antislavery newspapers or magazines before the Revolution. There was little of any sort of printed antislavery material, except occasional expositions, sermons, or remonstrances, published and privately distributed to small and select numbers of people, until the very eve of the Revolution. Neither were there established systems of recording and reporting court decisions or debates in colonial assemblies, so that taken in its entirety the period offers little to the historian in the way of documentary information. It offered less to the average citizen of that time in the way of enlightenment, intellectual stimulation, or persuasion. The man who opposed slavery did so, not because he had read a book, or newspaper, or otherwise digested an argument, but because he instinctively rejected a system of human relationships so utterly foreign to common decency. Roger Williams obviously was one

Dwight Lowell Dumond, *Antislavery: The Crusade for Freedom in America*. New York, NY: W.W. Norton & Company, Inc., 1961. Copyright © 1961 by the University of Michigan. Reproduced by permission.

of these people and so was Chief Justice Samuel Sewall, whose *The Selling of Joseph* (1700) was long thought to have been the first published argument against slavery in America. Nobody seems to have taken either one of them very seriously, but Sewall did state the first major indictment of slavery, one that was to be repeated a thousand times in every conceivable type of literature—the separation of men and women from their homeland, of husbands from wives, and of parents from children—and he touched lightly upon the evil effects of slavery upon the character of slaveholders.

THE QUAKERS AND SLAVERY

Sewall was a Puritan, and the Puritans were not the pioneers in the antislavery movement. That honor belongs to the Quakers, for the Quakers were gentle people, living by the precept of the golden rule, believing in the inherent dignity of man, the freedom of human will, and the equality of all men. They owned slaves in the seventeenth century and a part of the eighteenth, but George Fox sounded a warning against it in 1657. Thomas Drake says: "In this, his first discussion of slavery, he made only a beginning: he did not condemn slaveholding as such. But he did expound the idea of the equality of men in the eyes of God; and this idea—touchstone to the Truth—finally, more than a century later, freed the Quakers' slaves."

The Quakers experienced great difficulties from the beginning, for the defense of slavery by the suppression of freedom of inquiry and discussion and other civil rights, and by the use of charges of incendiarism and of foul invective to discredit the friend of the slave, did not originate in the American South, though it reached optimum heights there; nor did it develop in response to the violent language of abolitionists as has been claimed. It came out of the practice of slaveholding, the relationship between master and slave, the intoxication of unrestrained power, and the *habit* of destroying all opposition to the master's will. Furthermore, these early Quakers were not an obnoxious group of meddlers, talking of things they knew not of, any more than were the later antislavery leaders of the nineteenth century, as was charged and commonly believed then and now. They were slaveholders, rich and powerful slaveholders, in every part of British Colonial America, just as were many of the later antislavery leaders.

These Quakers abhorred all violence. They never spoke in harsh language. They opposed slavery from first to last on moral and religious grounds—as a sin. They made tremendous financial sacrifices to rid themselves of the contamination. They never asked anything for themselves by way of profit—political, social, or economic—from their friendship for the oppressed. Nevertheless, they were violently denounced, charged with inciting rebellion, suppressed, and finally driven out of Barbados because they sought to Christianize and educate their slaves. They were denied the poor privilege of freeing their slaves in the Southern states, and in the early congresses of the United States were accused of treason and incendiarism because they petitioned for the suppression of the African slave trade.

All of this came, of course, after they had steeled themselves for the ordeal through a century of soul-searching and consultation. The second Quaker protest was a letter of advice to Friends in America by William Edmundson, at Newport, Rhode Island, in 1676, and the third a "Remonstrance Against Slavery and the Slave-trade" by the Germantown (Pa.) Friends; but it is doubtful if more than a handful of people outside Quaker circles knew anything about them. The first printed protest was George Keith's *An Exhortation and Caution to Friends Concerning Buying or Keeping of Negroes* (1693), seven years before Samuel Sewall's *The Selling of Joseph*. It insisted upon the principle of brotherhood of all men and requested Friends to seek freedom for the slaves, to free their own slaves, and to lend assistance to fugitives. Whether it had any influence outside Quaker circles there is no way of knowing, but soul-searching had begun, and as early as 1698 Quakers were discussing their responsibility as slaveholders for the carnage in Africa and their responsibility to compensate slaves at the time of manumission both for labor while in bondage and as an aid to economic independence. This was not an easy road they chose nor a journey to be undertaken lightly.

They hesitated and drew back, and looked askance at those among them who became impatient with delay. In fact they disowned William Southeby and John Farmer, and then Ralph Sandiford and Benjamin Lay. Sandiford, who published *A Brief Examination of the Practice of the Times* (1729), was probably driven to his grave (he died in 1733 at age forty) by ostracism, and Benjamin Lay, who published *All Slave Keepers That Keep the Innocent in Bondage, Apostates* (1737), found no peace or comfort in even his most intimate human relationships.

TWO QUAKER LEADERS

Then came the two great leaders of pre-Revolutionary abolitionism—John Woolman, tailor, of New Jersey, and Anthony Benezet, schoolteacher, of Philadelphia. Woolman, whom Drake calls "the greatest Quaker of the eighteenth century and perhaps the most Christ-like individual that Quakerism has ever produced," traveled widely through Virginia and northward through Maryland, his own state of New Jersey, Pennsylvania, and New England. No other antislavery leader ever traveled as much, except Theodore Weld in the 1820's and 1830's, nearly a century later, and the two men were remarkably alike in their methods. Both labored mightily with individuals, though the later Presbyterian preached valiantly, and the earlier Quaker gently persuaded. What was the secret of Woolman's power? What gave Weld his tremendous influence over other men? We only know that Woolman was forever moving about. He wrote *Some Considerations on the Keeping of Negroes: Recommended to the Professors of Christianity of Every Denomination* in 1754, and a second part to the original in 1762. It was meant for the general public, not Friends alone, and it was the most widely distributed antislavery work before the Revolution. It still occupies an honored place upon the shelves of scholars. But it was this close, personal contact between Woolman and hundreds of slaveholders that was important, for the presence of the saint touches the souls of men more than a thousand printed pages influence their minds. It is one thing to listen to a sermon or read a book, and it is quite another thing to have a saintly person ask a man a question about personal conduct and then sit down with him in quiet meditation to think it over.

Woolman was a humanitarian in the finest sense of that term. He knew the truth, he spoke the truth, and men believed because they had no other choice. Wealth, war, and slavery were to him the three greatest enemies of the souls of men. He insisted that Christian doctrine embraced all men and that all men were entitled to freedom, but, above all, that no man was mentally or morally competent to rule others independent of restraints. Slavery was unchristian, it was unjust, it was cruel, and its effect upon owners and slaves alike was evil. Merely calling persons slaves created a false notion of natural inferiority, and "where slavekeeping prevails, pure religion and sobriety decline, as it evidently tends to harden the heart and render the soul less susceptible of that holy spirit of love, meakness, and charity, which is the peculiar character of a true Christian."

Benezet did not write as much as Woolman, and he wrote mostly about the slave trade, but he made perfectly clear that there was precious little difference between enslaving a man and holding him in slavery. His most important works were *A Caution and Warning to Great Britain and Her Colonies, in a Short Representation of the Calamitous State of the Enslaved Negroes in the British Dominions* (1766), and *Some Historical Account of Guinea, Its Situation, Produce, and the General Disposition of Its Inhabitants, with an Enquiry into the Rise and Progress of the Slave-Trade, Its Nature and Lamentable Effects* (1771). It was the latter pamphlet that inspired young Thomas Clarkson's interest in the cause. Much of his other printing was compilation, but he sent his pamphlets everywhere in America, England, and the continent of Europe, particularly to France, where he had been born in 1713, of Huguenot parentage. He corresponded widely with British leaders, particularly with Greenville Sharp, who represented Sommersett before Lord Mansfield, and with Thomas Clarkson whose works on the slave trade were reprinted and circulated in America. He was a friend of John Wesley, who copied his *Thoughts upon Slavery* almost verbatim from Benezet. Finally, he was a magnificent organizer, who channeled Quaker doctrine on slavery to the larger audience.

Whether Benezet was more important in the movement than Woolman is of little consequence. The works of both, along with the Bible, were the most precious possessions of every antislavery leader of the nineteenth century. They lived at the same time. The work of one complemented that of the other. They were friends and colleagues. Both exerted powerful influence in the movement. One was born in 1713, the other in 1720. Woolman, the mystic, died in England of smallpox in 1772. Benezet, the propagandist, died in 1764. One can only speculate on the terrible loss to the country at this critical period, for the real greatness of Benezet and Woolman, it seems to me, lies far beyond their emphasis upon the brotherhood of men and the inconsistency between slavery and Christianity— even beyond their persuasive power with slaveholders and their lifelong devotion to the cause.

FOUR GREAT TRUTHS

These men grasped four truths which were so basic in man's struggle for freedom as to be almost overpowering in their simplicity. Whether they came by way of revelation, or by agonizing mental concentration, the important thing is that they came to men who lived, and whose people lived, by the truth.

All men were equal in the sight of God. Slavery was a violation of the Christian principle of human brotherhood and the golden rule. There was no sanction for holding anyone in slavery in the Christian faith, and those who bought slaves and those who owned slaves were as guilty of the murderous warfare in Africa as if they were active participants.

This was a generation before the Revolution. Early Quaker literature was religious literature, and these men were working largely within the framework of a religious society. This ceased to be true when the Quakers had rid *themselves* of slavery, and at the time of the Revolution they contributed to the general emphasis upon the natural rights of man. When James Otis said in *The Rights of the British Colonies Asserted and Proved:* "The Colonists are by the law of nature free born, as indeed all men are, white or black," he was speaking the same language as Benezet. And Thomas Paine merely summed up the whole business in the concise fashion of an indictment in his *Slavery in America* (1775), when he said: "But to go to nations with whom there is no war, who have no way provoked, without farther design of conquest, purely to catch inoffensive people, like wild beasts, for slaves, is an height of outrage against Humanity and Justice, that seems left by Heathen nations to be practiced by pretended Christians ... As these people are not convicted of forfeiting freedom, they have still a natural, perfect right to it; and the Governments, whenever they come, should in justice set them free, and punish those who hold them in slavery ... Certainly one may, with as much reason and decency, plead for murder, robbery, lewdness, and barbarity as for this practice." The Quakers first abolished the practice of buying and selling of slaves. Buying a slave created a demand for another to be imported, thus stimulating the foreign slave trade ... directly implicating the purchaser in the African business. Buying was necessary to successful slaveholding operations because natural increase did not supply the losses, and abolishing the trade would ultimately abolish slavery. Probably, too, it was necessary to approach the final decision by degrees. In any case, buying and selling among them ceased in Philadelphia in 1758, London, England, in 1761, Maryland in 1768, New England in 1770, and New York in 1774. The abolition among them of slavery itself came more slowly, for various reasons, but it came, in the New England and Middle states before the close of the Revolution, and in Maryland and Virginia by 1788.

There was no basis whatever for doubting the mental and moral capacity of the Negroes to support themselves in a status of freedom as useful and creative members of society. Why there should have been any doubt about it when they had been taking care of themselves and the whites, too, for a long time, remains a mystery. Some people argued the point as a collateral issue to draw attention from the main idea of emancipation. With some it was a rationalization, but men of intelligence and honesty of purpose stumbled over it—Jefferson, for instance, Washington, and probably

Lincoln. Thousands joined in a movement to colonize the free Negroes in Africa or somewhere on this continent. The idea of biological inequality crystallized to the point where in my own time scholars have argued that Negroes who achieved greatly were of mixed blood, and literature of the most diabolical character depicting Negroes as apes is allowed to circulate freely.

The Quakers rejected all such nonsense. They set about educating their slaves for freedom. They established day schools for Negro children, Sabbath schools and evening schools (first and fifth day) for adults. They appointed committees of inspection to plan and advise the Negroes, committees of guardians to protect the orphans, committees on education, and committees for employment.

Whatever difficulties, problems, or necessary sacrifices might be connected with emancipation should be borne by those who were responsible for the outrage of slavery, not by the victims. There is record of a revealing letter from Patrick Henry to Robert Pleasants (1773) in which he said: "I am drawn along by the general inconvenience of living without them. I will not, I can not justify it. However culpable my conduct, I will so far pay my devoir to virtue, as to own the excellence and rectitude of her precepts, and to lament my own want of conformity to them." No Quaker was allowed such latitude of conduct. He freed his slaves. He was not allowed to take the easy way of selling them to someone else, or of freeing the children after a certain age as was later done by law. Financial ruin, abandonment of plantations, scorn and persecution by one's neighbors, migration to a city, a new state beyond the mountains—all of this, and more for many—such was the way of righteousness for those who had erred. None among them puts it quite as forcefully as Hugh H. Brackenridge in his brilliant satire, *Modern Chivalry* (1792): "It would greatly inconvenience thieves and cut-throats, who have run risks in acquiring skill in their profession, to be obliged all at once to desist from this and apply themselves to industry in other ways for a livelihood," but all understood the principle. They never countenanced economic arguments, either against slavery, or in defense of gradual emancipation. Some of them, like the families of

Warner Mifflin of Delaware and Robert Pleasants of Virginia, gave freedom to nearly one hundred slaves; and most of them left Virginia and the Carolinas for the new west.

Slaves were entitled to retributive justice. They must be compensated for work done while deprived of their freedom. Failure to educate and train them for responsible citizenship must be corrected. They must be assisted to economic independence. All of this by the man who owned them and must set them free. So well did they fulfill this obligation that in a reasonably short time there were two Negro schools in New York, seven in Philadelphia, one even in Alexandria, Virginia; and Negroes were building their own economy, establishing churches, and setting themselves up as tradesmen and skilled mechanics.

The Quakers had written a brilliant chapter in the moral progression of man. Other religious groups had failed at an earlier date to contest the political decision that Christians could be held as slaves *providing they were Negroes,* and they had failed fatally. They now agreed *in the slave country* that the whole question of slavery was a political question. They did not then, or later, do anything about it. In fact they threw the social teachings of Jesus out on the scrap heap and went along with the claim that slavery was a Christian institution.

A Virginian Lobbies the Virginia Legislature to End the Slave Trade

ARTHUR LEE

Although Arthur Lee was born into an aristocratic eighteenth-century Virginia slaveholding family, he grew morally opposed to slavery as a young man. In 1767, Lee voiced his opposition to slavery in a letter to the *Virginia Gazette*, calling slavery "a violation of justice and religion." His letter also condemned slave traders who obtained slaves in Africa by "violence, artifice & treachery." Lee's main purpose in writing was to convince the Virginia legislature to ban the importation of slaves into the colony, a goal that Lee did not achieve. The editor of the *Virginia Gazette* received widespread criticism for printing Lee's letter, and he chose not to publish a follow-up letter from Lee on the same subject.

T o Mr. Rind,
Sir—Permit me, in your paper, to address the members of our Assembly, on two points, in which the publick interest is very dearly concern'd.

The abolition of Slavery & the Retrieval of Specie, in this Colony, are the Subjects, on which I would bespeak their Attention. They are both to be accomplish'd by the same means.

Chosen as you are, Gentlemen, to watch over & provide for the publick weal and Welfare, whatever is offer'd, as tending to those desirable purposes, will I hope, meet from you a favourable

Arthur Lee, "Address on Slavery," *Virginia Gazette*, March 19, 1767.

ear. And, be the fate of my Sentiments as it will, I flatter myself that your pardon at least will be Indulged to the Writer.

SLAVERY VIOLATES JUSTICE AND RELIGION

Long and serious Reflection upon the nature & Consequences of Slavery, has Convinced me, that it is a Violation both of Justice and Religion; that it is dangerous to the safety of the Community in which it prevails; that it is destructive to the growth of arts & Sciences; and lastly, that it produces a numerous & very fatal train of Vices, both in the Slave, and in his Master. To prove these assertions, shall be the purpose of the following essay.

That Slavery, then, is a violation of Justice, will plainly appear when we consider what Justice is. It is simply & truly defin'd, as by Justinian, constans et perpetua voluntas jus suum cuique tribuendi, a constant Endeavour to give every man his right.

Now, as freedom is unquestionably the birth-right of all mankind, of Africans as well as Europeans, to keep the former in a State of slavery is a constant violation of that right, and therefore of Justice.

The ground on which the civillians, who favour Slavery, admit it to be just, Namely, Consent, force, and birth, is totally disputable. For surely a Man's own will or Consent, cannot be allow'd to introduce so important an innovation into society as that of Slavery, or to make himself an out-law, which is really the State of a Slave, since neither Consenting to nor aiding the Laws of ye Society, in which he lives, he is neither bound to obey them, nor entitled to their protection. To found any right in force, is to frustrate all right, and involve every thing in confusion, violence and rapine. With these two the last must fall, since if the Parent cannot be justly made a Slave, neither can the Child be born in Slavery.

"The law of nations," says Baron Montesquieu, "has doom'd prisoners to Slavery, to prevent their being Slain. The Roman civil law, permitted debtors whom their Creditors might treat ill, to Sell themselves. And the Law of nature requires that children, whom their parents, being Slaves, cannot maintain, should be slaves like them. These reasons of the Civillians are not just; it is not true that a Captive may be slain, unless in case of absolute necessity; but if he hath been reduced to slavery it is plain that no such necessity existed, since he was not slain.

It is not true that a freeman can sell himself. For sale supposes a price, but in this act the Slave & his property becomes immediately that of his Master, the slave therefore can receive no price, nor the Master pay &c. And if a man cannot sell himself, nor a prisoner of war be reduced to Slavery, much less can his Child." Such are the Sentiments of this illustrious civillian; his reasonings, which I have been oblidged to contract, the reader, interested in this subject, will do well to consult at large.

A CONDEMNATION OF THE SLAVE TRADE

Yet even these rights of impossition very questionable, nay, refutable as they are, we have not to authorize the Bondage of the Africans. For neither do they consent to be our Slaves, nor do we purchase them of their Conquerors. The British Merchants obtain them from Africa by violence, artifice & treachery, with a few trinkets to prompt those unfortunate & destestable people to enslave one another by force or Strategem. Purchase them indeed they may, under the authority of an act of British Parliment. An act entailing upon the Africans, with whom we were not at war, and over whom a British Parliment could not of right assume even a shadow of authority, the dreadfull curse of perpetual slavery upon them and their children forever. There cannot be in nature, there is not in all history, an instance in which every right of men is more flagrantly violated. The laws of the Antients never authorized the making slaves but of those nations whom they had conquer'd; yet they were Heathens and we are Christians. They were misled by a false and monstrous religion, divested of humanity, by a horrible & Barbarous worship; we are directed by the unering preceps of the revealed religion we possess, enlightened by its wisdom, and humanized by its benevolence. Before them were gods deformed with passions, and horrible for every cruelty &

Vice; before us is that incomparable pattern of Meekness, Charity, love, and justice to mankind, which so transcendently distinguished the founder of Christianity and his ever amiable doctrines. Reader—remember that the corner stone of your religion is to do unto others as you wou'd they shou'd do unto you; ask then your own Heart, whether it would not abhor anyone, as the most outrageous violator of this & every other principle of right, Justice & humanity, who should make a slave of you and your Posterity forever. Remember that God knoweth the heart. Lay not this flattering unction to your Soul, that it is the custom of the Country, that you found it so, that not your will, but your Necessity consents; Ah think, how little such an excuse will avail you in that awfull day, when your Saviour shall pronounce judgment upon you for breaking a law too plain to be misunderstood, too sacred to be violated. If we say that we are Christians, yet act more inhumanly and unjustly than Heathens, with what dreadfull justice must this Sentance of our blessed Saviours fall upon us: Not every one that sayeth unto me, Lord, Lord, shall enter into the Kingdom of Heaven; but he that doeth the will of my Father which is in heaven. Think a moment how much your temporal, your eternal wellfare, depends upon the abolition of a practice, which deforms the Image of your God; tramples on his reveal'd will, infringes the most Sacred rights, and violates humanity.

SLAVERY ENDANGERS THE STATE

Enough I hope has been said to prove that slavery is in violation of justice and religion. That it is dangerous to the safety of the State in which it prevails, may be as safely asserted.

What one's own experience hath not taught, that of others must decide. From hence does history derive its utility. For being, when truly written, a faithfull record of the transactions of mankind, and the consequences that flow'd from them; we are thence furnished with the means of judging what will be the probable effect of transactions similar among ourselves. We learn then from history, that slavery, wherever encouraged, has sooner or later been productive of very dangerous commotions.

I will not trouble my reader here with quotations in support of this assertion, but content myself with referring those, who may be dubious of its truth, to the histories of Athens, Lacedaemon, Rome, and Spain. And that this observation may bear its full weight, let me beg that it be remember'd these states were remarkable for being the most warlike in the world; the bravest and best trained to discipline and arms.

That we are not such is but too obvious. Yet it does not appear that the slaves in those Communitys, were so numerous as they are in ours. Demothenes during his orphanage, had been defrauded of a large fortune; and in his oration for retrieving it enumerates 52 Slaves. Tacitus, in mentioning a roman Nobleman, who was assassinated by one of his Slaves; records the whole number amounting to 400, to have suffered Death for that crime. From these facts we may conclude, that the proportion of slaves among the antients was not so great as with us; and as, notwithstanding this, the freemen, tho' infinitely better armed and disciplined than we are, were yet brought to the very brink of ruin by the insurrections of their Slaves; what powerfull reasons have not we, to fear even more fatal consequences from the greater prevalence of Slavery among us. How long how bloody and destructive, was the contest between the Moorish slaves and the native Spaniards, and after almost deluges of blood had been shed, the Spaniards obtain'd nothing more, than driving them into the mountains; from whence they remain themselves subjected to their perpetual inroads. Less bloody indeed, though not less alarming, have been the insurrections in Jamaica; and to imagine that we shall be forever exempted from this Calamity, which experience teaches us to be inseperable from slavery, so encouraged, is an infatuation as astonishing, as it will be surely fatal. On us, or on our posterity, the inevitable blow, must, one day, fall; and probably with the most irresistable vengeance the longer it is protracted. Since time, as it adds strength and experience to the slaves, will sink us into perfect security and indolence, which debillitating our minds, and enervating our bodies, will render us an easy conquest to the feeblest foe. Unarm'd already and undisciplined, with our Militia laws contemned, neglected or perverted, we are like the wretch at the feast; with a drawn sword depending over his head by a Single hair; yet we flatter ourselves, in opposition to the force of reason and conviction of experience, that the danger is not imminent.

To prosecute this Subject farther, at present, would I perceive Mr. Rind, engross too much of your paper, and most likely disgust the reader, I must therefore take leave to defer what remains to the next week. Happy shall I be if my poor attempts should prompt more able Heads to think and write upon a Subject, of such lasting import to the welfare of the Community. Strongly, I confess, am I attached to the positions here laid down, because they are formed upon long and serious deliberation; Yet I am open to that conviction, which truth ever operates on minds unseduced by Interest, and uninflamed by passion.

A Frenchman's View of American Slavery

J. HECTOR ST. JOHN DE CRÈVECOEUR

J. Hector St. John de Crèvecoeur was born in Caen, France, in 1735 and came to French Canada when he was nineteen years old. After serving as a French officer in the French and Indian War, Crèvecoeur remained in America for more than a decade and traveled widely. He recorded his observations of the American landscape in a series of descriptive essays that he collected and published under the title *Letters from an American Farmer* in 1782. Although Crèvecoeur generally described America and Americans very positively, his Letter IX, titled "Description of Charles Town," presented his readers with an aspect of America that he found troubling and distasteful: slavery. In this letter, Crèvecoeur contrasts the wealth and gaiety of Charles Town, South Carolina, with the wretched lives of black people living in bondage.

C harles-Town [South Carolina] is, in the north, what Lima is in the south; both are Capitals of the richest provinces of their respective hemispheres: you may therefore conjecture, that both cities must exhibit the appearances necessarily resulting from riches. Peru abounding in gold, Lima is filled with inhabitants who enjoy all those gradations of pleasure, refinement, and luxury, which proceed from wealth. Carolina produces commodities, more valuable perhaps than gold, because they are gained by greater industry; it exhibits also on our northern stage, a display of riches and luxury, inferior indeed to the former, but far superior to what are to be seen in our northern towns. Its situation is admirable, being built at the confluence of two large rivers, which receive in their course a great number of inferior streams; all navigable in the spring, for flat boats. Here

J. Hector St. John de Crèvecoeur, *Letters from an American Farmer*. New York: E.P. Dutton, 1957.

the produce of this extensive territory concentres; here therefore is the seat of the most valuable exportation; their wharfs, their docks, their magazines, are extremely convenient to facilitate this great commercial business. The inhabitants are the gayest in America; it is called the centre of our beau monde, and is always filled with the richest planters of the province, who resort hither in quest of health and pleasure. . . .

MASTERS AND SLAVES

While all is joy, festivity, and happiness in Charles-Town, would you imagine that scenes of misery overspread in the country? Their ears by habit are become deaf, their hearts are hardened; they neither see, hear, nor feel for the woes of their poor slaves, from whose painful labours all their wealth proceeds. Here the horrors of slavery, the hardship of incessant toils, are unseen; and no one thinks with compassion of those showers of sweat and of tears which from the bodies of Africans, daily drop, and moisten the ground they till. The cracks of the whip urging these miserable beings to excessive labour, are far too distant from the gay Capital to be heard. The chosen race eat, drink, and live happy, while the unfortunate one grubs up the ground, raises indigo, or husks the rice; exposed to a sun full as scorching as their native one; without the support of good food, without the cordials of any cheering liquor. This great contrast has often afforded me subjects of the most conflicting meditation. On the one side, behold a people enjoying all that life affords most bewitching and pleasurable, without labour, without fatigue, hardly subjected to the trouble of wishing. With gold, dug from Peruvian mountains, they order vessels to the coasts of Guinea; by virtue of that gold, wars, murders, and devastations are committed in some harmless, peaceable African neighbourhood, where dwelt innocent people, who even knew not but that all men were black. The daughter torn from her weeping mother, the child from the wretched parents, the wife from the loving husband; whole families swept away and brought through storms and tempests to this rich metropolis! There, arranged like horses at a fair, they are branded like cattle, and then driven to toil, to starve, and to languish for a few years on the different plantations of these citizens. And for whom must they work? For persons they know not, and who have no other power over them than that of violence, no other right than what this accursed metal has given them! Strange order of things! Oh, Nature, where art thou?—Are not these blacks thy children as well as we? On the other side, nothing is to be seen but the most diffusive misery and wretchedness, unrelieved even in thought or wish! Day after day they drudge on without any prospect of ever reaping for themselves; they are obliged to devote their lives, their limbs, their will, and every vital exertion to swell the wealth of masters; who look not upon them with half the kindness and affection with which they consider their dogs and horses. Kindness and affection are not the portion of those who till the earth, who carry the burdens, who convert the logs into useful boards. This reward, simple and natural as one would conceive it, would border on humanity; and planters must have none of it!

If negroes are permitted to become fathers, this fatal indulgence only tends to increase their misery: the poor companions of their scanty pleasures are likewise the companions of their labours; and when at some critical seasons they could wish to see them relieved, with tears in their eyes they behold them perhaps doubly oppressed, obliged to bear the burden of nature— a fatal present—as well as that of unabated tasks. How many have I seen cursing the irresistible propensity, and regretting, that by having tasted of those harmless joys, they had become the authors of double misery to their wives. Like their masters, they are not permitted to partake of those ineffable sensations with which nature inspires the hearts of fathers and mothers; they must repel them all, and become callous and passive. This unnatural state often occasions the most acute, the most pungent of their afflictions; they have no time, like us, tenderly to rear their helpless off-spring, to nurse them on their knees, to enjoy the delight of being parents. Their paternal fondness is embittered by considering, that if their children live, they must live to be slaves like themselves; no time is allowed them to exercise their pious office, the mothers must fasten them on their backs, and, with this double load, follow their husbands in the fields, where they too often hear no other sound than that of the voice or whip of the taskmaster, and the cries of their infants, broiling in the sun. These unfortunate creatures cry and weep like their parents, without a possibility of relief; the very instinct of the brute, so laudable, so irresistible, runs counter here to their master's interest; and to that god, all the laws of nature must give way. Thus planters get rich; so raw, so unexperienced am I in this mode of life, that were I to be possessed of a plantation, and my slaves treated as in general they are here, never could I rest in peace; my sleep would be perpetually disturbed by a retrospect of the frauds committed in Africa, in order to entrap them; frauds surpassing in enormity everything which a common mind can possibly conceive. I should be thinking of the barbarous treatment they meet with on ship-board; of their anguish, of the despair necessarily inspired by their situation, when torn from their friends and relations; when delivered into the hands of a people differently coloured, whom they cannot understand; carried in a strange machine over an ever agitated element, which they had never seen before; and finally delivered over to the severities of the whippers, and the excessive labours of the field. Can it be possible that the force of custom should ever make me deaf to all these reflections, and as insensible to the injustice of that trade, and to their miseries, as the rich inhabitants of this town seem to be? What then is man; this being who boasts so much of the excellence and dignity of his nature, among that variety of inscrutable mysteries, of unsolvable problems, with which he is surrounded? . . .

But is it really true, as I have heard it asserted here, that those blacks are incapable of feeling the spurs of emulation, and the cheerful sound of encouragement? By no means; there are a thousand proofs existing of their gratitude and fidelity: those hearts in which such noble dispositions can grow, are then like ours, they are susceptible of every generous sentiment, of every useful motive of action; they are capable of receiving lights, of imbibing ideas that would greatly alleviate the weight of their miseries. But what methods have in general been made use of to obtain so desirable an end? None; the day in which they arrive and are sold, is the first of their labours; labours, which from that hour admit of no respite; for though indulged by law with relaxation on Sundays, they are obliged to employ that time which is intended for rest, to till their little plantations. What can be expected from wretches in such circumstances? Forced from their native country, cruelly treated when on board, and not less so on the plantations to which they are driven; is there anything in this treatment but what must kindle all the passions, sow the seeds of inveterate resentment, and nourish a wish of perpetual revenge? They are left to the irresistible effects of those strong and natural propensities; the blows they receive, are they conducive to extinguish them, or to win their affections? They are neither soothed by the hopes that their slavery will ever terminate but with their lives; or yet encouraged by the goodness of their food, or the mildness of their treatment. The very hopes held out to mankind by religion, that consolatory system, so useful to the miserable, are never presented to them; neither moral nor physical means are made use of to soften their chains; they are left in their original and untutored state; that very state wherein the natural propensities of revenge and warm passions are so soon kindled. Cheered by no one single motive that can impel the will, or excite their efforts; nothing but terrors and punishments are presented to them; death is denounced if they run away; horrid delaceration if they speak with their native freedom; perpetually awed by the terrible cracks of whips, or by the fear of capital punishments, while even those punishments often fail of their purpose. . . .

A Scene of Horror

The following scene will I hope account for these melancholy reflections, and apologise for the gloomy thoughts with which I have filled this letter: my mind is, and always has been, oppressed since I became a witness to it. I was not long since invited to dine with a planter who lived three miles from——, where he then resided. In order to avoid the heat of the sun, I resolved to go on foot, sheltered in a small path, leading through a pleasant wood. I was leisurely travelling along, attentively examining some peculiar plants which I had collected, when all at once I felt the air strongly agitated, though the day was perfectly calm and sultry. I immediately cast my eyes toward the cleared ground, from which I was but at a small distance, in order to see whether it was not occasioned by a sudden shower; when at that instant a sound resembling a deep rough voice, uttered, as I thought, a few inarticulate monosyllables. Alarmed and surprised, I precipitately looked all round, when I perceived at about six rods distance something resembling a cage, suspended to the limbs of a tree; all the branches of which appeared covered with large birds of prey, fluttering about, and anxiously endeavouring to perch on the cage. Actuated by an involuntary motion of my hands, more than by any design of my mind, I fired at them; they all flew to a short distance, with a most hideous noise: when, horrid to think and painful to repeat, I perceived a negro, suspended in the cage, and left there to expire! I shudder when I recollect that the birds had already picked out his eyes, his cheek bones were bare; his arms had been attacked in several places, and his body seemed covered with a multitude of wounds. From the edges of the hollow sockets and from the lacerations with which he was disfigured, the blood slowly dropped, and tinged the ground beneath. No sooner were the birds flown, than swarms of insects covered the whole body of this unfortunate wretch, eager to feed on his mangled flesh and to drink his blood. I found myself suddenly arrested by the power of affright and terror; my nerves were convulsed; I trembled, I stood motionless, involuntarily contemplating the fate of this negro, in all its dismal latitude. The living spectre, though deprived of his eyes, could still distinctly hear, and in his uncouth dialect begged me to give him some water to allay his thirst. Humanity herself would have recoiled back with horror; she would have balanced whether to lessen such reliefless distress, or mercifully with one blow to end this dreadful scene of agonising torture! Had I had a ball in my gun, I certainly should have despatched him; but finding myself unable to perform so kind an office, I sought, though trembling, to relieve him as well as I could. A shell ready fixed to a pole, which had been used by some negroes, presented itself to me; I filled it with water, and with trembling hands I guided it to the quivering lips of the wretched sufferer. Urged by the irresistible power of thirst, he endeavoured to meet it, as he instinctively guessed its approach by the noise it made in passing through the bars of the cage. "Tankè, you whitè man, tankè you, putè somè poison and givè me." "How long have you been hanging there?" I asked him. "Two days, and me no die; the birds, the birds; aaah me!" Oppressed with the reflections which this shocking spectacle afforded me, I mustered strength enough to walk away, and soon reached the house at which I intended to dine. There I heard that the reason for this slave being thus punished, was on account of his having killed the overseer of the plantation. They told me that the laws of self-preservation rendered such executions necessary; and supported the doctrine of slavery with the arguments generally made use of to justify the practice; with the repetition of which I shall not trouble you at present.

CHAPTER 2

ABOLITIONISTS OF THE EARLY AMERICAN REPUBLIC

AMERICAN
SOCIAL
MOVEMENTS

Abolition and the American Revolution

MERTON L. DILLON

Merton L. Dillon, who taught in the history department at Ohio State University, is the author of biographies of two noteworthy American abolitionists, Elijah P. Lovejoy and Benjamin Lundy, and other books about American slavery. This selection is excerpted from *The Abolitionists: The Growth of a Dissenting Minority*, published in 1974. In it Dillon points out that during and after the American Revolution, many Americans began to sense a contradiction between their calls for liberty and equality and the institution of slavery. Antislavery Americans of the Revolutionary era embraced the concepts of natural law and natural rights—a philosophy that slavery negated. Key leaders of the American Revolution—Benjamin Franklin, John Adams, Alexander Hamilton, and even slave owners like George Washington and Thomas Jefferson—found slavery troubling during an era when Americans extolled liberty and equality.

S lavery was an institution whose growth in modern times was inseparable from the development of European empires in the New World. It first came under heavy and sustained attack when revolutionary upheaval racked the unity of one of those empires. This coincidence was not merely accidental.

For a few English colonials in America the intellectual currents that swept the Atlantic community in the mid-eighteenth century brought visions of a new and better world. Moral progress, those optimists believed, eventually could remove every age-old obstacle to happiness and virtue. Faith in human progress stimulated political revolt. While most of the Americans who chafed under English rule after the French and Indian

Merton L. Dillon, *The Abolitionists: The Growth of a Dissenting Minority*. DeKalb: Northern Illinois University Press, 1974. Copyright © 1974 by Northern Illinois University Press. All rights reserved. Reproduced by permission.

War doubtlessly had the easing of political control and the ending of economic restriction as their chief goal in opposing English policy, some took a larger view. They saw revolution as a more comprehensive process than merely the cutting of political ties and the removal of economic hobbles. Also encompassed within the term "revolution" was the dream that society could at last be freed from all those remnants of a less enlightened past that hampered the development of human potential. No American institution more strikingly belonged to that category than slavery.

It may be that white Americans in the 1760s were made more sensitive to English encroachments on their rights by their daily observation of what they themselves did to black men. Slavery was not simply a theoretical possibility, not a mere figure of speech. It was a state into which men actually had fallen. It was a condition observable within their own communities.

OPPOSITION TO SLAVERY IN COLONIAL AMERICA

Although Americans profited from slavery and had long taken its existence for granted, many now agreed that slavery violated natural law. This conclusion presented slaveholders of the Revolutionary era with a troublesome problem, because natural law had come to have for them much the same force that divine law exercised in earlier times. It was a rare politically-conscious American in the late eighteenth century who did not view slavery as conflicting with the natural-rights principles from which the Revolution was derived and as clashing with the Revolution's goals. That generally held assumption appeared unmistakably even in the rhetoric of the age.

By verbal association and analogy, discontented Americans compared their relation to England with the relation existing between slave and master. England, Americans charged, aimed to reduce free-born colonists to "slavery"; the political and economic regulations imposed by English officials "oppressed" Americans and threatened to "enslave" them. In justifying rebellion against such prospective dangers, Americans emphasized their inalienable right to freedom, drawing upon a venerable English radical tradition in the process. "We hold these truths to be self-evident," wrote Thomas Jefferson, "that all men are created equal; that they are endowed by their Creator with certain inalienable rights. . . ." By implication, Americans of the Revolutionary era extended the rights they claimed for themselves to all mankind.

A colonist needed no unusual degree of perception to note the embarrassing contradiction of a slaveholding people rebelling against "slavery." The crusty eighteenth-century English writer, Dr. Samuel Johnson, took delight in asking the obvious question: "How is it that we hear the loudest yelps for liberty among the drivers of negroes?" Americans too were uncomfortably aware of the irony in their situation. Some pious colonials construed the troubles they experienced with England as God's punishment imposed upon them for their own transgressions. Among those sins, it sometimes was said, slavery loomed the most prominent.

SLAVERY AND THE AMERICAN REVOLUTION

Thus in the Revolutionary era, a religiously inspired sense of guilt joined with a belief in the natural rights of man and faith in the dawning of an age of reason and benevolence to produce a home-grown critique of slavery.

Throughout America increasing numbers of the conscience-stricken, in the 1770s and afterward, freed their slaves, a procedure made easy even in the South when the legislatures of Delaware, Maryland, and Virginia removed restrictions that previously had either discouraged or prohibited such acts of generosity. In New England, slaves themselves shared the liberating enthusiasm of the time and petitioned the state legislatures to grant them freedom. Not surprisingly, their efforts in Massachusetts apparently were aided by Samuel Adams, one of the earliest and most consistent advocates of colonial rights. In several Northern states and in Virginia, antislavery legislators introduced bills providing for gradual emancipation. Only in South Carolina and Georgia were evidences of advancing antislavery sentiment for the most part lacking.

On account of such events, opponents of slavery during the Revolutionary era understandably viewed themselves as forming part of the great army of Americans whose activities in behalf of liberty were combining to usher in a more enlightened age. They had no reason whatever to consider their antislavery program as being out of harmony with the main developments of their time. On the contrary, society everywhere was apparently moving toward greater freedom and the loosening of bonds. Accordingly, abolitionists might reasonably anticipate that the continued working of moral progress would soon accomplish their aims with minimal opposition and conflict.

The most prominent figures of the American Revolution were also leaders in the expression of antislavery sentiment. Benjamin Franklin was founder and president of the Pennsylvania Abolition Society. Alexander Hamilton wrote powerful statements asserting the natural equality of Blacks and their right to freedom. John Dickinson, Thomas Jefferson, George Washington, Patrick Henry, John Adams, Henry Laurens, George Mason, James Otis—all those Revolutionary leaders and others of lesser fame—let it be known by words and sometimes by their actions that they gave at least some support to the movement against slavery

Abolitionists of the Revolutionary period thus enjoyed the assurance that comes to those who know they have friends and partisans both in high places and scattered generally throughout the land. It had not always been so, and, as we shall see, the relation between active opponents of slavery and the rest of society would soon undergo drastic change.

OPPOSITION TO SLAVERY: A MINORITY SENTIMENT

When, toward the end of the seventeenth century—several generations before the outbreak of the American Revolution—opposition to slavery was first conspicuously voiced in America, it obviously was minority sentiment that could find no means to influence the direction of events. Antislavery in those early years was the expression of individual dissent. It did not represent the considered views of significant portions of the population; moreover, no channels then existed by which such minority sentiment could exert influence or even be widely heard.

In the early colonial period it was an unawareness that slavery presented any moral problem rather than an active resistance to antislavery ideas that provided the chief obstacle to the spread of antislavery sentiment. There was as yet no imperative to act, for no widespread dissatisfaction with existing social practices and institutions had developed. Concepts of liberty seldom appeared in the writings of a people who did not yet feel themselves oppressed. . . .

QUAKER OPPOSITION TO SLAVERY

Until well into the nineteenth century, Quakers dominated the antislavery movement, furnishing an important part of the rank-and-file membership as well as some of antislavery's most effective leaders. Even after actual antislavery leadership had passed to other hands, traditions that were closely associated with Quaker thought and practice—especially the doctrine of non-resistance—continued to exercise significant influence among abolitionists.

The tides of antislavery sentiment that swept America during the Revolutionary era suggested that influential segments of the population had come to share at least part of the Quaker hostility to slavery. In the North, antislavery ideology became strong enough to counteract the economic interest some Northerners had in slavery and to overcome the racially inspired apprehensions commonly felt about the results of freeing Blacks. Although in New York and Pennsylvania, efforts for abolition aroused strong and stubborn resistance, gradual emancipation was accepted even in those states. In 1804, the process was completed in the North when New Jersey, the last to fall in line, enacted a gradual emancipation law.

No legislature south of Pennsylvania passed such a measure. Yet this fact did not signify a dearth of antislavery sentiment in the South. Especially in Maryland and Virginia the numbers of freed Negroes rapidly increased as individual owners manumitted their slaves, themselves voluntarily doing what the legislatures of their states refused to require.

Religious institutions, like the political institutions, were beginning to take antislavery stands. By emphasizing the worth and potential of every individual—whatever his earthly status—and his equality before God, the revivalism of the Great Awakening of the 1740s encouraged antislavery thought and action within the churches (though it hardly required them). Revivalism as a process provided a model for the personal decision and commitment that came to characterize those abolitionists whose inspiration was predominantly religious. Further, the theology that developed in several Protestant groups in the middle of the eighteenth century counseled "disinterested benevolence toward mankind," a duty that some converts expressed in antislavery action. The church organizations themselves, however, while often officially condemning slavery, were extremely reluctant to impose sanctions against their slaveholding members.

ANTISLAVERY MOVEMENTS

By the late eighteenth century, enlightened opinion everywhere supported antislavery movements, and antislavery sentiment had been channeled into both politics and religion. Thus, at the end of the Revolutionary era abolitionists anticipated the future with confidence. Both religious principle and political ideals had been marshaled to the support of their program. Abolitionists understood very well that the victories they had achieved were far from conclusive and that much entrenched interest and inertia with respect to slavery still needed to be overcome; nevertheless, impressive evidence suggested that the nation was moving steadily toward the ultimate elimination of slavery. It would have been easy to conclude that continued work for that end, following lines already established, could achieve success.

Reformers might have tempered their optimism had they recognized the import of two forces that emerged soon after "independence" to work powerfully against their efforts. One of these was economic—a growing absorption with the accumulation of wealth and a strengthening attachment to individual property rights, rights often considered fully as "natural" and "inalienable" as any other secured by the Revolution. Abolitionism was sometimes opposed as being in conflict with such economic rights and interests.

RACIAL IDEOLOGY

The other force countering abolition was cultural—a sharpening awareness of the significance of racial differences. Race consciousness, perhaps never absent from Anglo-American culture, had contributed to the ease with which Blacks in America were enslaved in the seventeenth century. Historians Winthrop Jordan and David Brion Davis have demonstrated that at the end of the eighteenth century it also worked against their emancipation. White Americans, struggling after independence to develop a national identity, embraced the conviction that America was intended exclusively for Whites. Despite the fact that they had never been alone on the continent but from practically the first day of settlement shared occupation with both Indians and Blacks, Anglo-Americans assumed that Providence designed America to be a white man's country. The possibility that Blacks would be incorporated into American society as free men, thereby "debasing" it and destroying its homogeneity, must accordingly be resisted; above all, racial amalgamation must not be allowed to occur.

While some critics of slavery fully shared such views, abolitionists invariably rejected them. When Thomas Jefferson in his *Notes on the State of Virginia* (1785) expressed carefully qualified and tentative doubts about the intellectual potential of Blacks and about their fitness to remain in America after emancipation, advocates of abolition vigorously contradicted him. They denied that the alleged inferiority was inherent. But these strong, twentieth-century-like assertions of human equality had little effect in countering the more widely held and more deeply ingrained contrary views.

Early abolitionists at first underestimated the power of such racist ideas and economic interests to obstruct the progress of antislavery principles. They expected to persuade southern political majorities to enact the same kind of gradual emancipation laws that had ended slavery in Pennsylvania, New York, and New Jersey. Gradualism and moderation would characterize both their program and their mode of operation before 1830. Though they mercilessly condemned slavery and slaveholders and looked forward to total abolition, they seldom proposed drastic, immediate change in master-slave relations. They were more likely to regard slavery as an evil to be ameliorated and very gradually ended through slow and painless changes than as a sin to be abandoned immediately. As men of the Enlightenment, they were conscious of the fragility of the ties that bind men and institutions together. As observers of contemporary events they were dismayed by the violence that accompanied the French Revolution and the slave upheavals in Santo Domingo. Thus they feared the violent disruption of the entire social order that might result from precipitate change in any part of it. Accordingly, in developing their programs they were more likely than their nineteenth-century successors to consider the interests and prejudices of slaveholders and to weigh the consequence of abolition on the whole of society.

Even great evils, they assumed, should be remedied by good will and moderate efforts and through mutual consent. They had confidence in gradualism, in the efficacy of piecemeal reform. Patience was a virtue many of them deliberately cultivated, for they confidently expected Providence eventually to provide solutions for problems that then seemed beyond the powers of man to resolve. Meanwhile, through rational accommodation, mankind could gradually progress in social relations and thereby move step-by-step toward a better world. He could ameliorate such evils as slavery and gradually, with minimal disruption to the social order, eliminate them altogether. That goal could be reached through rational persuasion and mutual adjustment without resorting to the clash of conflicting interests.

Such caution and restraint and such conciliatory attitudes were not qualities for which nineteenth-century abolitionists would be noted. The dramatic transformation that soon took place in abolitionist temper and mode of operation resulted in part from a change in world view from the rationality of the Enlightenment, with its sense of corporate order, to the more impatient and emotional Romantic age, with its emphasis on the needs, aspirations, and worth of the individual. In part, the changed attitudes and tactics of the abolitionists can be accounted for simply as resulting from their own prolonged, frustrating experience as reformers.

Abolitionists at the Constitutional Convention

CATHERINE DRINKER BOWEN

Catherine Drinker Bowen is the author of *Miracle at Philadelphia*, the definitive study of the Philadelphia Convention of 1787, which resulted in the formation of the United States Constitution. In this excerpt from that text, Bowen recounts a discussion among the convention delegates on slavery. Many delegates were vehemently antislavery, seeing the institution as a blatant contradiction of the principles articulated in the Declaration of Independence. Some southern delegates, however, defended slavery as vital to their region's economy. In the end, Bowen suggests, the delegates set aside the moral issues surrounding slavery and reached a political solution to the problem of slavery that allowed both the North and the South to ratify the new Constitution.

The question before the [Constitutional] Convention was not, Shall slavery be abolished? It was rather, Who shall have power to control it—the states or the national government? As the Constitution now stood, Congress could control the traffic in slaves exactly as it controlled all other trade and commerce.

Yet always when the question came up, members spoke out bluntly and with feeling upon the basic moral issue. Roger Sherman said he looked on the slave trade as "iniquitous," but he did not think himself bound to make opposition. Gouverneur Morris declared slavery to be a "nefarious institution, the curse of heaven on the states where it prevailed." Travel through the whole continent! declaimed Morris angrily. Compare the free regions, their "rich and noble cultivation . . . with the misery and poverty which overspreads the barren wastes of Virginia, Maryland and the other states having slaves." Must the North then send its militia to defend the South against such an institution, should the need arise and slaves rebel against their masters? "Wretched Africans!" exclaimed Morris. "The vassalage of the poor has ever been the favorite offspring of aristocracy!"

This was bold talk. Gouverneur Morris, once launched and on his feet—wooden leg, stout cane, flashing eye—seldom stopped short of his oratorical goal.

Proslavery Voices

[John] Rutledge said flatly that religion and humanity had nothing to do with the question. "Interest alone is the governing principle of nations." The eighteenth century seldom deceived itself concerning the governing principles of rulers or nations; Rutledge did not speak ironically. He meant to turn the discussion from the rights of human beings to the conveniences of trade and commerce, and he succeeded. The true question, Rutledge said, was "whether the Southern states shall or shall not be parties to the Union." Let the North consult its interest and it would not oppose the increase of slaves to harvest commodities of which it would become the carrier. [Oliver] Ellsworth of Connecticut suggested the decision be left to the states severally: "What enriches a part enriches the whole, and the states are the best judges of their particular interest." Moreover the old Confederacy had not meddled with this point; Ellsworth saw no necessity for bringing it within the policy of the new one. Charles Pinckney said brusquely that South Carolina would not agree to any government which prohibited the slave trade. And if the states were left at liberty, South Carolina by degrees would probably "do of herself what is wished."

It is the perennial catchword: leave the states to themselves and they will be good, they will prove themselves exemplary members of the American family. George Mason, however, would have none of this. On the twenty-second of August he rose to make his famous speech, brought on by Roger Sherman's saying again that though he disapproved the slave trade, abolition seemed to be proceeding gradually. The good sense of the several states would probably by degrees complete it; Sherman thought best to leave the matter as they found it, and not create more objections to the new government.

A Southerner Condemns Slavery

Mason was in an excellent position to have his say and be listened to by his Southern colleagues. It was common knowledge that his magnificent plantation employed two hundred slaves and that their master would long ago have freed them had it been possible. "This infernal traffic," Mason began, "originated in the avarice of British merchants! The British government constantly checked the attempts of Virginia to put a stop to it."

How much of this statement delegates were ready to accept, one cannot judge. It was all too reminiscent of [Thomas] Jefferson's diatribe in his rough draft of the Declaration of Independence: the "King of Great Britain kept open a market where *men* were bought and sold, and prostituted his negative by suppressing Virginia's legislative attempts to restrain this execrable commerce." (Before adopting the Declaration, Congress struck out every word of this.) But Mason now used the old argument confidently, then went on to speak of slavery not in terms of expedience—" interest," commerce, ships, profit—but in a high moral tone. Slaves, he said, "produce the most pernicious effect on manners. Every master of slaves is born a petty tyrant; they bring the judgment of heaven on a country. . . . Slavery discourages arts and manufactures. The poor despise labor when they see it performed by slaves. . . . The Western people," said Mason indignantly, "are already calling out for slaves for their new lands, and will fill that country with slaves if they can be got through South Carolina and Georgia. I hold it essential in every point of view that the general government should have power to prevent the increase of slavery. . . . I lament," said Mason earnestly, "that some of our Eastern brethren [New Englanders] have from a lust of gain embarked on this nefarious traffic."

The shaft struck home; shipowning delegates were at once on the defensive. Oliver Ellsworth declared icily that as he had never owned a slave he could not judge the effects of slavery on character, and that if the matter must be considered in a moral light, we should go further and free the slaves already in the country. Had not abolition already taken place in Massachusetts? Connecticut was making provision for so doing.

A MORAL DEFENSE OF SLAVERY

Young Charles Pinckney here voiced the only moral defense of slavery that was expressed in Convention. The institution was justified by the example of all the world, he said, as witness Greece, Rome and the sanction given by the modern states of France, Holland and England. "In all ages," said Pinckney, "one half of mankind have been slaves. If the Southern states were let alone" (again the argument), they would "probably of themselves stop importation."

General Charles Cotesworth Pinckney immediately bolstered his cousin and fellow Carolinian by declaring that even if he himself and all his colleagues agreed to the new government on such terms, they would never obtain the consent of their constituents: "South Carolina and Georgia cannot do without slaves." Abraham Baldwin of Georgia wished the matter left to the states, to which James Wilson coolly replied that if Georgia and South Carolina were as disposed to get rid of the slave traffic in as short a time as had been suggested, they would never refuse to enter the Union merely because importation might be prohibited. John Dickinson with his impressive manner came out for national control of the question. He "considered it as inadmissible on every principle of honor and safety that the importation of slaves should be authorized to the states by the Constitution. The true question was whether the national happiness would be promoted or impeded by the importation, and this question ought to be left to the national government, not to the states particularly interested." As to the arguments about Greece and Rome, those states were made unhappy by their slaves; moreover, both England and France excluded slaves from their kingdoms.

A POLITICAL SOLUTION

Rufus King said the problem should be considered "in a political light only." Langdon of New Hampshire was strenuous for giving the power of prohibition to the general government. He could not, he said, in good conscience leave it to the states. Rutledge declared the people of the Carolinas and Georgia would "never be such fools as to give up so important an interest." Roger Sherman said it was better to let the Southern states import slaves than to part with these states, "if they make that a *sine qua non.*"

In the end a compromise was reached: the Constitution would permit the importation of slaves until the year 1808, after which time it would be forbidden. Thus far, Mason and Dickinson had won their point: a matter that concerned the public good should be transferred from local to central authority, from state to Congress. No delegate had come to Philadelphia hoping for anything so drastic as to outlaw slavery from the United States, even those who hated it most. This was not a legislative body, to make laws. It was the business of delegates to create a Constitution for the country as it existed, and if slavery made a mockery of the words freedom, liberty, the rights of man, then those who thought so could have their say on the floor.

Without disrupting the Convention and destroying the Union they could do no more. The time was not yet come.

A Founding Father's Critique of Slavery

BENJAMIN FRANKLIN

Benjamin Franklin was arguably the most famous American of the late-eighteenth century—a renowned international diplomat, the greatest American inventor and scientist of his era, a skilled writer, and a political theorist without whom the thirteen British colonies might never have gained independence or formed a republic. Although Franklin once owned a slave, he came to detest the institution as a violation of a fundamental American principle—the right to rise from poverty and obscurity to wealth and fame, as he himself had done so impressively. In March 1790, Franklin read in the *Federal Gazette* that a southern congressman had criticized his colleagues for attempting to meddle with the institution of slavery. The next day, Franklin, using the pen name Historicus, wrote a letter to the editor of the *Gazette* in which he presented a devastating critique of slavery. Franklin recorded a speech by a member of the fictional Divan of Algiers, who justified his enslavement of Christians with the same arguments used by southerners who defended American slavery.

S ir,
    Reading last night in your excellent Paper the speech of Mr. Jackson in Congress against their meddling with the Affair of Slavery, or attempting to mend the Condition of the Slaves, it put me in mind of a similar One made about 100 Years since by Sidi Mehemet Ibrahim, a member of the Divan of Algiers, which may be seen in Martin's Account of his Consulship, anno 1687. It was against granting the Petition of the Sect called *Erika*, or Purists, who pray'd for the Abolition of Piracy and Slavery as being unjust. Mr. Jackson does not quote it; perhaps he has not

Benjamin Franklin, "On the Slave-Trade," *The Federal Gazette*, March 1790.

seen it. If, therefore, some of its Reasonings are to be found in his eloquent Speech, it may only show that men's Interests and Intellects operate and are operated on with surprising similarity in all Countries and Climates, when under similar Circumstances. The African's Speech, as translated, is as follows.

A Speech on Slavery

"Allah Bismillah, &c. God is great, and Mahomet is his Prophet.

"Have these *Erika* considered the Consequences of granting their Petition? If we cease our Cruises against the Christians, how shall we be furnished with the Commodities their Countries produce, and which are so necessary for us? If we forbear to make Slaves of their People, who in this hot Climate are to cultivate our Lands? Who are to perform the common Labours of our City, and in our Families? Must we not then be our own Slaves? And is there not more Compassion and more Favour due to us as Mussulmen, than to these Christian Dogs? We have now above 50,000 Slaves in and near Algiers. This Number, if not kept up by fresh Supplies, will soon diminish, and be gradually annihilated. If we then cease taking and plundering the Infidel Ships, and making Slaves of the Seamen and Passengers, our Lands will become of no Value for want of Cultivation; the Rents of Houses in the City will sink one half; and the Revenues of Government arising from its Share of Prizes be totally destroy'd! And for what? To gratify the whims of a whimsical Sect, who would have us, not only forbear making more Slaves, but even to manumit those we have.

"But who is to indemnify their Masters for the Loss? Will the State do it? Is our Treasury sufficient? Will the *Erika* do it? Can they do it? Or would they, to do what they think Justice to the Slaves, do a greater Injustice to the Owners? And if we set our Slaves free, what is to be done with them? Few of them will return to their Countries; they know too well the greater Hardships they must there be subject to; they will not embrace our holy Religion; they will not adopt our Manners; our People will not pollute themselves by intermarrying with them. Must we maintain them as Beggars in our Streets, or suffer our Properties to be the Prey of their Pillage? For Men long accustom'd to Slavery will not work for a Livelihood when not compell'd. And what is there so pitiable in their present Condition? Were they not Slaves in their own Countries?

"Are not Spain, Portugal, France, and the Italian states govern'd by Despots, who hold all their Subjects in Slavery, without Exception? Even England treats its Sailors as Slaves; for they are, whenever the Government pleases, seiz'd, and confin'd in Ships of War, condemn'd not only to work but to fight, for small Wages, or a mere Subsistence, not better than our Slaves are allow'd by us. Is their Condition then made worse by their falling into our Hands? No; they have only exchanged one Slavery for another, and I may say a better; for here they are brought into a Land where the Sun of Islamism gives forth its Light, and shines in full Splendor, and they have an Opportunity of making themselves acquainted with the true Doctrine, and thereby saving their immortal Souls. Those who remain at home have not that Happiness. Sending the Slaves home then would be sending them out of Light into Darkness.

WHAT MUST BE DONE ABOUT THE SLAVES?

"I repeat the Question, What is to be done with them? I have heard it suggested, that they may be planted in the Wilderness, where there is plenty of Land for them to subsist on, and where they may flourish as a free State; but they are, I doubt, too little dispos'd to labour without Compulsion, as well as too ignorant to establish a good government, and the wild Arabs would soon molest and destroy or again enslave them. While serving us, we take care to provide them with every thing, and they are treated with Humanity. The Labourers in their own Country are, as I am well informed, worse fed, lodged, and cloathed. The Condition of most of them is therefore already mended, and requires no further Improvement. Here their Lives are in Safety. They are not liable to be impress'd for Soldiers, and forc'd to cut one another's Christian Throats, as in the Wars of their own Countries. If some of the religious mad Bigots, who now teaze us with their silly Petitions, have in a Fit of blind Zeal freed their Slaves, it was not Generosity, it was not Humanity, that mov'd them to the Action; it was from the conscious Burthen of a Load of Sins, and Hope, from the supposed Merits of so good a Work, to be excus'd Damnation.

"How grossly are they mistaken in imagining Slavery to be disallow'd by the Alcoran [Koran]! Are not the two Precepts, to quote no more, 'Masters, treat your Slaves with kindness; Slaves, serve your Masters with Cheerfulness and Fidelity,' clear Proofs to the contrary? Nor can the Plundering of Infidels be in that sacred Book forbidden, since it is well known from it, that God has given the World, and all that it contains, to his faithful Mussulmen, who are to enjoy it of Right as fast as they conquer it. Let us then hear no more of this detestable Proposition, the Manumission of Christian Slaves, the Adoption of which would, by depreciating our Lands and Houses, and thereby depriving so many good Citizens of their Properties, create universal Discontent, and provoke Insurrections, to the endangering of Government and producing general Confusion. I have therefore no doubt, but this wise Council will prefer the Comfort and Happiness of a whole Nation of true Believers to the Whim of a few *Erika*, and dismiss their Petition."

SLAVERY WILL CONTINUE

The Result was, as Martin tells us, that the Divan came to this Resolution; "The Doctrine, that Plundering and Enslaving the Christians is unjust, is at best *problematical;* but that it is the Interest of this State to continue the Practice, is clear; therefore let the Petition be rejected."

And it was rejected accordingly.

And since like Motives are apt to produce in the Minds of Men like Opinions and Resolutions, may we not, Mr. Brown, venture to predict, from this Account, that the Petitions to the Parliament of England for abolishing the Slave-Trade, to say nothing of other Legislatures, and the Debates upon them, will have a similar Conclusion? I am, Sir, your constant Reader and humble Servant,

HISTORICUS.

A Plan for the Abolition of Slavery

FERNANDO FAIRFAX

In 1790, as the United States Congress discussed the slave trade and other issues relating to slavery, Fernando Fairfax, a Virginian, offered a plan for the gradual emancipation of American slaves. At the time, the United States capital was seated in Philadelphia, and Fairfax published his plan in a Philadelphia periodical titled *American Museum* in December 1790. Fairfax's plan is the first published abolition plan in America. Fairfax proposed that freed African Americans should be settled in a special colony in Africa protected by the United States government, that slave owners who freed their slaves should be compensated, and that the freed slaves should be properly educated. Colonization plans like Fairfax's were discussed for another seventy years. Several thousand American former slaves migrated to Liberia in Africa during the nineteenth century. After the Civil War, colonization plans were shelved as freed slaves became United States citizens.

This subject has afforded, in conversation, a wide field for argument, or rather, speculation, both to the friends and opposers of emancipation. Whilst the former plead natural right and justice, which are considered as paramount to every other consideration: the latter insist upon policy, with respect both to the community and to those who are the objects proposed to be benefited: the one party considers liberty as a natural right, which we cannot, without injustice, withhold from this unhappy race of men: the other, at the same time that it admits these principles, opposes a general emancipation, on account of the inconveniencies which would result to the community and to the slaves themselves, and which, consequently, would ren-

Fernando Fairfax, "Plan for Liberating the Negroes Within the United States," *American Museum*, December 1790.

der it impolitic; besides the injustice which would be done to individuals by a legislative interference (without voluntary consent) in private property, which had been acquired and possessed under the laws of the country. But no practicable scheme has yet been proposed, which would unite all these principles of justice and policy, and thereby remove all ground for opposition: all that has hitherto been offered to the public upon this subject, has been addressed, rather to the feelings, than to the cool and deliberate judgment. The following plan is therefore submitted, without apology, since it is only intended to suggest the idea, which may be improved by some abler hand.

A Plan for Gradual Emancipation

It seems to be the general opinion, that emancipation must be gradual; since, to deprive a man, at once, of all his right in the property of his negroes, would be the height of injustice, and such as, in this country, would never be submitted to: and the resources of government are by no means adequate to making at once a full compensation. It must therefore be by voluntary consent—consequently in a gradual manner. It is equally agreed, that, if they be emancipated, it would never do to allow them *all* the privileges of citizens: they would therefore form a separate interest from the rest of the community. There is something very repugnant to the general feelings, even in the thought of their being allowed that free intercourse, and the privilege of intermarriage with the white inhabitants, which the other freemen of our country enjoy, and which only *can* form one common interest. The remembrance of their former situation, and a variety of other considerations, forbid this privilege—and as a proof, where is the man of all those who have liberated their slaves, who would marry a son or a daughter to one of them? and if *he* would not, who would? So that these preju dices, sentiments, or whatever they may be called, would be found to operate so powerfully as to be insurmountable. And though the laws should allow these privileges, yet the same effect would still be produced, of forming a separate interest from the rest of the community; for the laws cannot operate effectually against the sentiments of the people.

If this separate interest of so great a number in the same community, be once formed, by any means, it will endanger the peace of society: for it cannot exist between two neighbouring states, without danger to the peace of each—How much less, then, between the inhabitants of the same country?

PROPOSITIONS

This suggests the propriety, and even necessity of removing them to a distance from this country. It is therefore proposed,

That a colony should be settled, under the auspices and protection of congress, by the negroes now within the united states, and be composed of those who already, as well as those who, at any time hereafter, may become liberated by the voluntary consent of their owners; since there are many who would willingly emancipate their slaves, if there should appear a probability of their being so disposed of, as neither to injure themselves nor the community. As an additional inducement, government may, as the resources of the country become greater, offer a reward or compensation, for emancipation. There is, however, in the mean time, a sufficient number to form a very considerable colony.

That congress should frame a plan, and appoint the proper officers for the government of the colony in its infant state, until the colonists should themselves become competent to that business.

That there should be suitable provision made for their support and defence. And

That, to forward their progress in the useful arts, and to qualify them for the business of legislation; a considerable number of those who are intended to be sent over after the first settlement, should be properly educated and instructed; and that one of the first objects should be the establishment of seminaries in the colony for a like purpose.

That the seat of this colony should be in Africa, their native climate, as being most suitable for the purposes intended. They will there be at such a distance as to prevent all the before-mentioned inconveniences of intercourse, &c. at the same time that they are situated within the neighbourhood of other nations of the same kind of people, with whom they may, after a little time, maintain the most intimate intercourse without any inconvenience. They will still have a great superiority over their neighbours, on account of their knowledge in the several useful arts, and as they gradually advance in importance, will, by their influence, diffuse this knowledge among this rude race of men. Nor ought we to consider as of little importance, the tendency that this settlement would have, to spreading a knowledge of the Christian religion among so great a proportion of mankind, who are at present ignorant of it—and that too in the most effectual manner.

With respect to ourselves, we might reap every advantage that we could enjoy from the settlement of any other colony— if not more. They would require our support and protection for a short time only with fewer supplies of necessaries than any other (from the nature of the climate). And they might soon, from their industry, and by commercial intercourse, make us ample amends for our expenses, and be enabled to live without our protection; and, after some time, to become an independent nation. But if we should gain no advantages, we should still accomplish the object intended

COUNTERING OBJECTIONS TO THE PLAN

Many difficulties and objections may be urged against this plan; but none, that are not equally forcible against the first planting of any other colony; and had they been fully admitted, neither this country, nor any other colony, would ever have been settled.

It may be said, that England, not long since, made an experiment of this kind, which was found not to succeed. But this can, by no means, be admitted as decisive: the number they sent over, was very small, compared to what we should be able to send: and perhaps, the means they adopted were incompetent to the accomplishment of the object. But did not the same thing occur in the first settlement of Virginia? There were two attempts made, before they succeeded; nor did the colony, at last, begin to flourish, until proper encouragements were given to industry, by the prospect presented to each man, individually, of receiving the reward of this industry, by commercial intercourse with other countries, and by the benefit which would result immediately to himself or to his family. This is confirmed by a circumstance recorded in the history of this colony, viz. when they first began to labour for subsistance, the plan was, that the produce of each man's labour, should be put into the common stock, from whence all should be supplied as occasion required. The consequence was, that they never made enough for their support, and were once or twice near starving; but as soon as each man had his own ground assigned him, with directions to maintain himself and family, they made a plenty.

It may, however, be urged, that the negroes (having contracted such dispositions for idleness as always to require compulsion) will never voluntarily labour for subsistence. It is granted, that this would be the case, were they to remain among us, where they find other means of support, and where they may prey upon others: and it is even probable, that, for a little time after their removal, the force of habit would operate in a considerable degree. But there can be no doubt, but that the same circumstances, which have once influenced mankind in any situation, will, in the same situation, actuate them again. And let us consult human nature—we shall find, that no man would labour but through necessity, or, after this necessity is answered, without some stimulus to honour or grandeur, either to himself or to his posterity: and that there is hardly any man who will not, from some of these motives, be induced to industry, if placed in a situation where there is no other resource.

All these motives are now wanting to the people in question: but who can say that when, by a change of situation, they shall operate in their full force, they will not have their effect?

A Call for Abolition by the First American Antislavery Society

THE AMERICAN CONVENTION FOR PROMOTING THE ABOLITION OF SLAVERY AND IMPROVING THE CONDITION OF THE AFRICAN RACE

The American Convention for Promoting the Abolition of Slavery and Improving the Condition of the African Race, the first national antislavery society established in America, formed in 1794. Between its establishment and 1829, the American Convention met twenty-four times. State antislavery societies from New York, Pennsylvania, New Jersey, and other states sent delegates to the national society, which kept detailed minutes of its proceedings. In 1804, the American Convention released this call for the gradual abolition of slavery in the United States. The document conceded that "many inconveniences may result from a general liberation of the People of Colour" but that the continuance of slavery in the United States would result in even more serious problems and would jeopardize the future prosperity of the United States.

A principal object of our concern, is to rouse the attention of the public to the continued—may we not say—increasing necessity of exertion. We fear many have taken up an idea, that there is less occasion now than formerly, for active zeal in promoting the cause of the oppressed African: but when it is remembered that there are about nine hundred thousand slaves in our country! that hundreds of vessels do annually sail from our shores, to traffic in the blood of our fellow men! and

The American Convention for Promoting the Abolition of Slavery and Improving the Condition of the African Race, *Address . . . to the People of the United States*. Philadelphia: Solomon W. Conrad, 1804.

that the abominable practice of kidnapping is carried on to an alarming extent! surely it will not be thought a time for supineness and neglect. Ought not rather every faculty of the mind to be awakened? and in a matter wherein the reputation and prosperity of these United States are so deeply involved, is it possible that any can remain as indifferent and idle spectators?

The gross and violent outrages committed by a horde of kidnappers, call aloud for redress. We have reason to believe, there is a complete chain of them along our sea coast, from Georgia to Maine. Like the vulture, soaring in apparent indifference, while watching for his prey, these shameless men, disguised in the habiliments of gentlemen, haunt public places, and at night seize and carry off the victims of their avarice. The Convention are informed of some of their insidious manoeuvres. They generally have vessels moored in small rivers and creeks, and af-

A Condemnation of the Slave Trade

Olaudah Equiano was a slave, born in Africa around 1745 and transported to America as a child, who gained his freedom in 1766 and later became literate. At the time of the American Revolution, he was actively involved in the British antislavery movement. Equiano's specific target of protest was the international slave trade. In his autobiography, The Interesting Narrative of the Life of Olaudah Equiano, or Gustavus Vassa, the African, Written by Himself, *published in 1789, Equiano presents a vivid description of the horrid conditions aboard the slave vessel that brought him to America.*

The stench of the hold while we were on the coast was so intolerably loathsome, that it was dangerous to remain there for any time, and some of us had been permitted to stay on the deck for fresh air; but now that the whole

ter stealing the unprotected, they decoy by stratagem and allure by specious offers of gain, such free persons of colour as they find susceptible of delusion. Others residing near the sea coast, are continually purchasing slaves in the middle states, to sell at an advanced price to their compeers in infamy. For the victims of this shocking business, they find a ready market among the southern planters. The design of this detail, must be obvious: It is to excite the vigilance of every friend to humanity and to virtue, in the detection and punishment of these monsters in the shape of men.

To complain of injuice, or petition for redress of grievances, cannot be mistaken for rebellion against the laws of our country. We lament therefore the existence of statutes in the state of North Carolina, prohibiting individuals the privilege of doing justice to the unfortunate slave, and to their own feelings, by set-

ship's cargo were confined together, it became absolutely pestilential. The closeness of the place, and the heat of the climate, added to the number in the ship, which was so crowded that each had scarcely room to turn himself, almost suffocated us. This produced copious perspirations, so that the air soon became unfit for respiration, from a variety of loathsome smells, and brought on a sickness among the slaves, of which many died, thus falling victims to the improvident avarice, as I may call it, of their purchasers. This wretched situation was again aggravated by the galling of the chains, now become insupportable; and the filth of the necessary tubs [toilets], into which the children often fell, and were almost suffocated. The shrieks of the women, and the groans of the dying, rendered the whole a scene of horror almost inconceivable.

Olaudah Equiano, *The Interesting Narrative of the Life of Olaudah Equiano, or Gustavus Vassa, the African, Written by Himself.* New York: W.W. Norton, 2001.

ting him at liberty; and we learn with the deepest regret, that the state of South Carolina has recently repealed the law prohibiting the importation of slaves from Africa into that state. Such appears to be the melancholy fact; but we cannot restrain the involuntary question—Is this possible? Is the measure of iniquity not yet filled? Is there no point at which you will stop? Or was it necessary to add this one step, to complete the climax of folly, cruelty, and desperation? Oh legislators! we beseech you to reflect, before you increase the evils which already surround you in gloomy and frightful perspective!

Abolition Is a Humane Cause

Beholding with anxiety the increase rather than diminution of slavery and its dreadful concomitants, we earnestly request the zealous co-operation of every friend to justice and every lover of his country. It is an honourable, a virtuous, and a humane cause in which we have embarked. Much good has already been effected, but much remains to be done; and, under the divine blessing, may we not confidently hope, that in proportion to the sincerity of our motives, and the temperate, firm, and persevering constancy of our exertions, will be our success, and peaceful reward. Those who live contiguous to the sea-ports, in particular, we wish may be stimulated to vigilance, that none of those shameful acts of atrocity adverted to, may elude deserved punishment; and our fellow citizens of the eastern states are respectfully invited to pay attention to the clandestine traffic in slaves, carried on from some of their ports. Such daring infractions of the laws of our country require prompt and decisive measures.

Many aspersions have been cast upon the advocates of the freedom of the Blacks, by malicious or interested men; but, conscious of the rectitude of our intentions, and the disinterestedness of our endeavours, we hope not to be intimidated by censure from performing the part assigned to us. We frankly own, that it is our wish to promote a general emancipation; and, in doing this, it is our belief we essentially promote the true interests of the state: Although many inconveniencies may result from a general liberation of the People of Colour; yet those which flow from their continuance in slavery, must be infinitely greater, and are everyday increasing. It is, therefore, in our estimation, desirable that this object should be brought about with as much speed as a prudent regard to existing circumstances, and the safety of the country, will admit: But in all our endeavours for its accomplishment, we hope to move with care and circumspection. We pointedly disavow the most distant intention to contravene any existing law of the states collectively or separately—We will not knowingly infringe upon the nominal rights of property, although those rights may only be traced to our statute-books; and while we desire to be supported in our endeavours to defend the cause of the oppressed, we hope that discretion and moderation will characterize all our proceedings. We feel with others the common frailties of humanity, and, therefore cannot expect an exemption from error. The best intentions are sometimes inadvertently led astray; a lively zeal in a good cause may occasionally overleap the bounds of discretion: although therefore individuals may, in some instances, have suffered their zeal to exceed knowledge, yet we repeat, that the line of conduct which we approve, and which is consonant with the spirit and design of our institutions, is in strict conformity with a due submission to existing laws, and to the legal claims of our fellow citizens. On this ground we think we have a just claim to the countenance and support of all liberal minds—of all who delight in the real prosperity of their country, and in the multiplication of human happiness.

We conclude in the expression of a hope, that the Supreme Disposer of events, will prosper our labours in this work of justice, and hasten the day, when liberty shall be proclaimed to the captive, and this land of boasted freedom and independence, be relieved from the opprobrium which the sufferings of the oppressed African now cast upon it.

CHAPTER 3

THE FORMATION OF A NATIONAL ABOLITIONIST MOVEMENT

AMERICAN
SOCIAL
MOVEMENTS

Slavery Violates the Will of God

DAVID WALKER

David Walker, an African American who was born free in North
Carolina in 1785, moved to Boston as a young man and became involved in that city's budding abolitionist movement. He worked on
Freedom's Journal, the first newspaper in the United States published
by and for African Americans, and he frequently lectured on the evils
of slavery at antislavery rallies and meetings. In 1829, Walker published
an antislavery pamphlet titled *David Walker's Appeal*, one of the first
abolitionist texts authored by an African American. The pamphlet
was reprinted several times and distributed widely. This excerpt from
David Walker's Appeal highlights the religious foundation of Walker's
critique of American slavery. A year after his *Appeal* was published,
Walker died under mysterious circumstances.

I will give here a very imperfect list of the cruelties inflicted
on us by the enlightened Christians of America.—First, no
trifling portion of them will beat us nearly to death, if they find
us on our knees praying to God,—They hinder us from going
to hear the word of God—they keep us sunk in ignorance, and
will not let us learn to read the word of God, nor write—If
they find us with a book of any description in our hand, they
will beat us nearly to death—they are so afraid we will learn to
read, and enlighten our dark and benighted minds—They will
not suffer us to meet together to worship the God who made
us—they brand us with hot iron—they cram bolts of fire down
our throats—they cut us as they do horses, bulls, or hogs—they
crop our ears and sometimes cut off bits of our tongues—they
chain and hand-cuff us, and while in that miserable and

David Walker, *David Walker's Appeal, in Four Articles; Together with a Preamble, to the Coloured
Citizens of the World, but in Particular, and Very Expressly, to Those of the United States of America*, edited by Charles M. Wiltse. New York: Hill and Wang, 1965.

wretched condition, beat us with cow-hides and clubs—they keep us half naked and starve us sometimes nearly to death under their infernal whips or lashes (which some of them shall have enough of yet)—They put on us fifty-sixes and chains, and make us work in that cruel situation, and in sickness, under lashes to support them and their families.—They keep us three or four hundred feet under ground working in their mines, night and day to dig up gold and silver to enrich them and their children.—They keep us in the most death-like ignorance by keeping us from all source of information, and call us, who are free men and next to the Angels of God, their property! ! ! ! ! ! They make us fight and murder each other, many of us being ignorant, not knowing any better.—They take us, (being ignorant,) and put us as drivers one over the other, and make us afflict each other as bad as they themselves afflict us—and to crown the whole of this catalogue of cruelties, they tell us that we the (blacks) are an inferior race of beings! incapable of self government! !—We would be injurious to society and ourselves, if tyrants should loose their unjust hold on us! ! ! That if we were free we would not work, but would live on plunder or theft! ! ! ! that we are the meanest and laziest set of beings in the world! ! ! ! ! That they are obliged to keep us in bondage to do us good! ! ! ! ! !—That we are satisfied to rest in slavery to them and their children! ! ! ! ! !—That we ought not to be set free in America, but ought to be sent away to Africa! ! ! ! ! ! ! ! —That if we were set free in America, we would involve the country in a civil war, which assertion is altogether at variance with our feeling or design, for we ask them for nothing but the rights of man, viz. for them to set us free, and treat us like men, and there will be no danger, for we will love and respect them, and protect our country—but cannot conscientiously do these things until they treat us like men.

Slave Owners Have Offended God

How cunning slave-holders think they are! ! !—How much like the king of Egypt who, after he saw plainly that God was determined to bring out his people, in spite of him and his, as powerful as they were. He was willing that Moses, Aaron and the Elders of Israel, but not all the people should go and serve the Lord. But God deceived him as he will Christian Americans, unless they are very cautious how they move. What would have become of the United States of America, was it not for those among the whites, who not in words barely, but in truth and in deed, love and fear the Lord?—Our Lord and Master said:—"[But] Whoso shall offend one of these little ones which believe in me, it were better for him that a millstone were hanged about his neck, and that he were drowned in the depth of the sea." But the Americans with this very threatening of the Lord's, not only beat his little ones among the Africans, but many of them they put to death or murder. Now the avaricious Americans, think that the Lord Jesus Christ will let them off, because his words are no more than the words of a man! ! ! In fact, many of them are so avaricious and ignorant, that they do not believe in our Lord and Saviour Jesus Christ. Tyrants may think they are so skillful in State affairs is the reason that the government is preserved. But I tell you, that this country would have been given up long ago, was it not for the lovers of the Lord. They are indeed, the salt of the earth. Remove the people of God among the whites, from this land of blood, and it will stand until they cleverly get out of the way.

I adopt the language of the Rev. Mr. S.E. Cornish, of New York, editor of the Rights of All, and say: "Any coloured man of common intelligence, who gives his countenance and influence to that colony, further than its missionary object and interest extend, should be considered as a traitor to his brethren, and discarded by every respectable man of colour. And every member of that society, however pure his motive, whatever may be his religious character and moral worth, should in his efforts to remove the coloured population from their rightful soil, the land of their birth and nativity, be considered as acting gratuitously unrighteous and cruel."

Let me make an appeal brethren, to your hearts, for your cordial co-operation in the circulation of "The Rights of All," among us. The utility of such a vehicle conducted, cannot be estimated. I hope that the well informed among us, may see the absolute necessity of their co-operation in its universal spread among us. If we should let it go down, never let us undertake any thing of the kind again, but give up at once and say that we are really so ignorant and wretched that we cannot do any thing at all! !—As far as I have seen the writings of its editor, I believe he is not seeking to fill his pockets with money, but has the welfare of his brethren truly at heart. Such men, brethren, ought to be supported by us. . . .

GOD WILL DELIVER US

The Americans may say or do as they please, but they have to raise us from the condition of brutes to that of respectable men, and to make a national acknowledgement to us for the wrongs they have inflicted on us. As unexpected, strange, and wild as these propositions may to some appear, it is no less a fact, that unless they are complied with, the Americans of the United States, though they may for a little while escape, God will yet weigh them in a balance, and if they are not superior to other men, as they have represented themselves to be, he will give them wretchedness to their very heart's content.

And now brethren, having concluded these four Articles, I submit them, together with my Preamble, dedicated to the Lord, for your inspection, in language so very simple, that the most ignorant, who can read at all, may easily understand—of which you may make the best you possibly can. Should tyrants take it into their heads to emancipate any of you, remember that your freedom is your natural right. You are men, as well as they, and instead of returning thanks to them for your freedom, return it to the Holy Ghost, who is our rightful owner. If they do not want to part with your labours, which have enriched them, let them keep you, and my word for it, that God Almighty, will break their strong band. Do you believe this, my brethren?—See my Address, delivered before the General Coloured Association of Massachusetts, which may be found in Freedom's Journal, for Dec. 20, 1828.—See the last clause of that Address. Whether you believe it or not, I tell you that God will dash tyrants, in combination with devils, into atoms, and will bring you out from your wretchedness and miseries under these *Christian People! ! ! ! ! !*

Those philanthropists and lovers of the human family, who have volunteered their services for our redemption from wretchedness, have a high claim on our gratitude, and we should always view them as our greatest earthly benefactors.

If any are anxious to ascertain who I am, know the world, that I am one of the oppressed, degraded and wretched sons of Africa, rendered so by the avaricious and unmerciful, among the whites.—If any wish to plunge me into the wretched incapacity of a slave, or murder me for the truth, know ye, that I am in the hand of God, and at your disposal. I count my life not dear unto me, but I am ready to be offered at any moment. For what is the use of living, when in fact I am dead. But remember, Americans, that as miserable, wretched, degraded and abject as you have made us in preceding, and in this generation, to support you and your families, that some of you, (whites) on the continent of America, will yet curse the day that you ever were born. You want slaves, and want us for your slaves! ! ! My colour will yet, root some of you out of the very face of the earth! ! ! ! ! ! You may doubt it if you please. I know that thousands will doubt—they think they have us so well secured in wretchedness, to them and their children, that it is impossible for such things to occur.

So did the antideluvians doubt Noah, until the day in which the flood came and swept them away. So did the Sodomites doubt, until Lot had got out of the city, and God rained down fire and brimstone from Heaven upon them, and burnt them up. So did the king of Egypt doubt the very existence of a God; he said, "who is the Lord, that I should let Israel go?" Did he not find to his sorrow, who the Lord was, when he and all his mighty men of war, were smothered to death in the Red Sea? So did the Romans doubt, many of them were really so ignorant, that they thought the whole of mankind were made to be slaves to them; just as many of the Americans think now, of my colour. But they got dreadfully deceived. When men got their eyes opened, they made the murderers scamper. The way in which they cut their tyrannical throats, was not much inferior to the way the Romans or murderers, served them, when they held them in wretchedness and degradation under their feet. So would Christian Americans doubt, if God should send an Angel from Heaven to preach their funeral sermon. The fact is, the Christians having a name to live, while they are dead, think that God will screen them on that ground.

See the hundreds and thousands of us that are thrown into the seas by Christians, and murdered by them in other ways. They cram us into their vessel holds in chains and in handcuffs—men, women and children, all together! ! O! save us, we pray thee, thou God of Heaven and of earth, from the devouring hands of the white Christians! ! ! . . .

In conclusion, I ask the candid and unprejudiced of the whole world, to search the pages of historians diligently, and see if the Antideluvians—the Sodomites—the Egyptians—the Babylonians—the Ninevites—the Carthagenians—the Persians—the Macedonians—the Greeks—the Romans—the Mahometans—the Jews—or devils, ever treated a set of human beings, as the white Christians of America do us, the blacks, or Africans. I also ask the attention of the world of mankind to the declaration of these very American people, of the United States.

William Lloyd Garrison Commences Publication of the *Liberator*

On January 1, 1831, William Lloyd Garrison began publishing the *Liberator*, the most successful and influential abolitionist newspaper in American history. Garrison established the *Liberator* after an earlier abolitionist paper on which he worked in Baltimore, *Genius of Universal Emancipation*, folded and after he had a falling out with a Boston newspaper editor. The historian Henry Mayer, in an excerpt from his book *All on Fire: William Lloyd Garrison and the Abolition of Slavery*, describes the planning that Garrison undertook to launch that newspaper and assesses its impact on the nation during its thirty-five-year run. According to Mayer, Garrison made Americans listen to the abolitionist argument in a way that his predecessors had not.

With the *Transcript* now closed to him, [William Lloyd] Garrison intensified his efforts to acquire a forum of his own. His interest in Washington, D.C., had waned over his weeks of touring New England, where "contempt [seemed] more bitter, opposition more active, detraction more relentless, prejudice more stubborn, and apathy more frozen" than he had anticipated. Garrison lacked experience in the capital, but he knew the Boston printing trade and had grown absorbed by the challenge the city presented. If Dr. [Lyman] Beecher could walk in the Pilgrims' footsteps, Garrison reasoned, he himself could

Henry Mayer, *All on Fire: William Lloyd Garrison and the Abolition of Slavery*. New York: St. Martin's Press, 1998. Copyright © 1998 by Henry Mayer. All rights reserved. Reproduced by permission of St. Martin's Press, LLC.

FORMATION OF A NATIONAL ABOLITIONIST MOVEMENT • 103

follow the revolutionary path of [John] Adams and [James] Otis and inspire a moral reformation in the shadow of Faneuil Hall.

STARTING THE LIBERATOR

Garrison first talked over his freshly invigorated idea for *The Boston Public Liberator* with his circle of friends, who had tried unsuccessfully to launch a local antislavery society. Collier thought he could find Garrison some space in Merchants' Hall, where so many of the benevolent papers were issued. Isaac Knapp, his boyhood chum and predecessor at the *Free Press*, volunteered to give Garrison some help at the case, and Stephen Foster, their friend at the *Christian Watchman*, thought he could print the work in spare hours at his press until Garrison could buy a secondhand one of his own. The editor next talked to his small cadre of well-connected admirers. Samuel J. May agreed with Garrison that New England's insensibility was a "moral phenomenon" that ought to be addressed directly from Boston, as did his cousin Samuel Sewall, whose namesake and ancestor had written one of the earliest-known antislavery tracts, *The Selling of Joseph*, in 1700. Another of May's Harvard classmates, David L. Child, who had fought in Spain against the Bourbon monarch and endured two libel prosecutions for his newspaper attacks upon Jacksonian politicians, encouraged Garrison's venture from his post as editor of the *Massachusetts Journal*, the very first newspaper on which Garrison had worked in Boston. Child's wife, the prominent author Lydia Maria Child, whom Garrison admired for her humanitarian views and fiction sympathetic toward Indians and slaves, at first thought the idea was too provocative, but soon came around, deciding that "it would take live fish to swim upstream."

For all his goodwill, however, the circumspect Sewall also worried about giving unnecessary offense. A name like *Public Liberator*, with its evocation of [Simón] Bolívar and the South American revolutions on the one hand and the Irish defiance of Daniel O'Connell on the other, might be too readily construed as an invitation to slave rebellion. Wouldn't a milder name, perhaps *The Safety Lamp*, more accurately reflect the editorial philosophy and intentions? Garrison did not agree. He meant his paper to concentrate public attention upon the slaves' liberation, and he meant to uphold a universal standard of freedom. Indeed, he planned to subjoin to the title (which would be *The Liberator*, with no city name affixed) the motto "Our Country is the World—Our Countrymen are Mankind." With a boldness quite striking for one dependent upon subsidies, Garrison made it plain that the conduct of the paper would be his alone, and with a deference not always apparent in benefactors Sewall accepted the editor's judgment.

GAINING THE SUPPORT OF BLACKS

The firm support of a handful of strong-minded rebels among the elite, however, would not be enough. Having learned in Baltimore how significant the black community could be in sustaining a radical newspaper, Garrison would not begin *The Liberator* until he had gained the confidence of black Bostonians. Compared to Baltimore's 15,000 blacks or Philadelphia's 22,000, the black population of Boston—1,875, according to the 1830 census—seemed minuscule, but for Garrison they stood large as the living embodiment of the cause. The city had always had a black presence. The ship *Desire* had landed a parcel of slaves along with a cargo of tobacco in 1638; the western end of the Copps Hill burial ground contained the graves of generations of black mariners and domestic workers, both slave and free; a black sailor, Crispus Attucks, had fallen in the Boston "massacre" of 1770; a black minuteman, Peter Salem, had killed the redcoats' Major Pitcairn on Bunker Hill; a black domestic servant, Phyllis Wheatley, who had been baptized in Old South, had received a commendation from General Washington for her patriotic verses. Just before the Revolution, the town's 1,500 blacks (whose freedom was confirmed by Massachusetts constitutional enactments in 1780) had accounted for nearly ten percent of the town's population, but by Garrison's time, the spectacular growth of the city had reduced the black segment to only three percent of the total.

Black people lived on the margins of Boston municipal life.

Though eligible to vote, they stood excluded from juries and the militia and found themselves confined to the lower echelon of available jobs. Seasonal laborers, such as black dockworkers and sailors, lived close to the wharves, in large boardinghouses that functioned as fraternal associations and social clubs. Workers with steadier jobs, such as sawyers, teamsters, cooks and maids, or those with valet-related occupations such as barbers, hairdressers, seamstresses, laundresses, and clothes merchants, tended to leave the rowdy North End for the upcoming West End, where small row houses on the north slope of Beacon Hill afforded two or three families shared dwelling space. (When a man married and left one of the North End halls, his friends termed him "lost to the hill.") The families on "the hill" had founded a Baptist church on Belknap Street, a Methodist church on May Street, and a temperance boardinghouse on Southac Street, though these reputable establishments could not overmatch the gaming houses and bordellos on nearby Buttolph and Cambridge streets that provided less savory income opportunities for the neighborhood. "The hill" was not a ghetto, however. Some black families, especially mulattos of Caribbean ancestry, with a little more property than the other, lived quietly on streets south of the commercial center, and white artisans also took advantage of the cheap housing in the spreading West End.

The black community took care of itself. Its grocers served as informal bankers; its social clubs, which dated back to the African Society of 1796, brought food and firewood to the sick; its barbershops became bulletin boards; and the African Society's Meeting House (where the Baptists worshipped and a school for black youth flourished) became the community's town hall. Although Boston had a tolerant reputation, black people faced racial abuse, the indignities of segregated schools and churches, and a citizenship decidedly second-class if not as precarious as that endured by their counterparts in Baltimore, where the legal machinery of slavery might readily entrap them again. Yet leaders in Boston's black community felt confident enough to raise their voices politically, not only against slavery, but against the prejudiced conditions of their own lives. In 1826, Boston took the lead in forming the General Colored Association of Massachusetts as both a philanthropic and protest organization, and in 1826, David Walker had used the association's forum to articulate the position that later formed the basis of his visionary pamphlet. In August 1830, however, Walker—a robust man in his midthirties—died, apparently of a lung disease that also claimed his baby daughter, but the loss was devastating enough to generate community suspicions that he had been a victim of foul play. No evidence could be found to substantiate the charge, and the police would not take up the case.

William Lloyd Garrison

When Garrison made overtures to the black community five months later, no one else had come forward to speak or publish as forcibly as Walker had. Nor had anyone come forward with a plan for a black-run newspaper, for Boston's small black population could not have sustained a venture by itself even if the city's printing trades had not shut out people of color. (Walker had his pamphlet printed clandestinely in New York and had served as the Boston agent for Samuel Cornish's newspapers, *Freedom's Journal* and *The Rights of All*, which had gone out of business.)

Garrison had a ready access to "the hill" through two preacher friends, his landlord, William Collier, and his mother's beloved pastor, John Peak, who had come to Boston to share with Collier the task of ministering to the black Baptist congregation until the vacancy in its pulpit created by the resignation of its founding pastor, the Rev. Thomas Paul, could be filled. The ailing Paul—along with his Methodist counterpart, the Rev. Samuel Snowden—blessed Garrison's endeavor. The two black ministers, indeed, had called out hearty amens during the editor's talk at the Athenaeum, and Paul had warmly embraced the young man at the lectern afterward.

On December 10, 1830, two days before Garrison's twenty-fifth birthday, he spoke to a group of black leaders and expressed his deep sympathy for those "struggling against wind and tide," as he always put it, to advance their rights and defend their character. Garrison often said that he never rose to address a black audience without feeling ashamed of his own color, and he hoped that he could atone for the wrongs done to blacks by devoting his life to the struggle for liberty and equal citizenship. He intended his newspaper to support them in maintaining self-respect, educating their children, fighting for their constitutional rights, and organizing an assault upon the monstrous and tyrannical slave system. Such forthrightness and simplicity won him many friends that night. One of the meeting's organizers, James G. Barbadoes, a hairdresser whose name bespoke his West Indian origins, later praised him for remarks "full of virtue and consolation . . . [that] furnished a rule to live by and die by." Ever since Garrison's imprisonment in Baltimore, Barbadoes said, he had known the editor to be "God's servant," and he expressed gratitude that this young man had not perished in the South, but had been spared to bring his "precious fruit" to the benefit of Boston. Although some leaders, notably the Masons' John T. Hilton, nursed suspicions born of long experience, most of the activists followed Barbadoes in regarding the young printer as "a Daniel come to judgment." They would make the newspaper their own, and a committee of black women headed by Elizabeth Riley and Bathsheba Fowler began to raise a few dollars to support it.

PREPARING THE FIRST ISSUE

Garrison decided to go ahead with a "specimen number"—printer's lingo for a sample—which he intended to publish on New Year's Day, 1831. Relying upon the "truck and dicker" system, he and Knapp gathered their equipment and traded their manual labor for office space and some case and press time at Foster's *Christian Watchman* in Merchants' Hall. Knapp canvassed for supplies: potash and lime for cleaning type, lamp oil, and charcoal for ink, brushes and rollers and blotters, baskets for papers and twine for bundling stacks for the post office. Garrison, who would have sole billing as editor though he shared the publisher's title with Knapp, began the task of typesetting copy and composing the pages. By the end of December 1830, Garrison had made ready an issue of four pages, with four columns laid out neatly on a modest fourteen-by-nine page. He faced only one more obstacle: a lack of paper.

The partners had hoped that Deacon Moses Grant, a paper supplier and a fellow in the temperance movement, would extend them a few reams on credit, but Grant declined. He knew them to be reputable, the story went; he worried less about his money than about the fanatical notions they proposed to advance—he wanted no part of those. The project seemed stalled until Knapp found another firm that would advance a small quantity of paper on seven days' credit. They went ahead with the press run, assuming that money somehow would turn up in time. On the day the bill was due Garrison went to the post office and found a check for fifty-four dollars from James Forten, the black leader from Philadelphia, who asked the editor to consider the money as advance payment for twenty-seven subscriptions. Names and addresses were carefully enclosed, along with Forten's ardent hopes that Garrison's efforts to combat slavery and prejudice would not be in vain. The editor had appealed to Forten a few days after the meeting with Boston's black leaders, and he always credited the wealthy sailmaker's prompt and generous response with making *The Liberator* a reality.

THE FIRST ISSUE COMES OFF THE PRESS

On the afternoon of Saturday, January 1, 1831, the first issue came off the press. Block capital letters proclaimed THE LIBERATOR across the banner. The front page offered a poetic salutation, reports on the campaign to abolish slavery in the District of Columbia, and the customary address "To the Public," which Garrison turned into an editorial manifesto. In August he had issued proposals for establishing a journal in Washington, D.C., he said, but the enterprise "was palsied by public indifference." Having become convinced that the free states, especially New England, required "a greater revolution in public sentiment" than he had previously realized, he would now "lift up the standard of emancipation in the eyes of the nation, *within sight of Bunker Hill and in the birth place of liberty.*"

Judging it unnecessary to republish his August manifesto, Garrison emphasized only his reliance on the Declaration of Independence and a nonsectarian intention to enlist all religions and parties in "the great cause of human rights." He would "strenuously contend for the immediate enfranchisement of our slave population," Garrison promised, and he repudiated what he called his "unreflecting" assent to the "popular but pernicious doctrine of *gradual* abolition" that he had expressed at Park Street Church in July, 1829. "I seize this opportunity to make a full and unequivocal recantation," he wrote, "and thus publicly ask pardon of my God, of my country, and of my brethren the poor slaves, for having uttered a sentiment so full of timidity, injustice and absurdity."

The Liberator, he promised, would make slaveholders and their apologists tremble. He would redeem the nation's patriotic creed by making "every statue leap from its pedestal" and rouse the apathetic with a trumpet call that would "hasten the resurrection of the dead." He would speak God's truth "in its simplicity and power," and he would speak severely. He would also speak from the heart, in his own voice and in the first person singular rather than the more distant and aloof editorial plural. "I *will be* as harsh as truth, and as uncompromising as justice," Garrison pledged. "On this subject I do not wish to think or speak, or write, with moderation. No! No! Tell a man whose house is on fire to give a moderate alarm . . . but urge me not to use moderation in a cause like the present." He drove the point home with staccato phrases: "I am in earnest—I will not equivocate—I will not excuse—I will not retreat a single inch." Then he reached into the upper case and added one more promise: "—AND I WILL BE HEARD."

Thus began one of the most remarkable ventures in the history of American journalism. No editor has ever produced a newspaper of agitation for longer than Garrison sustained *The Liberator*, which appeared weekly without interruption for thirty-five years and did not cease publication until the ratification of the Thirteenth Amendment constitutionally abolished slavery in December 1865. When the twenty-five-year-old Garrison started his newspaper, Abraham Lincoln was a twenty-one-year-old sodbuster on the Illinois prairie, Jefferson Davis was a newly commissioned U.S. Army officer fighting the Sauk and Fox on the Wisconsin frontier, and Davis's West Point classmate Robert E. Lee was building federal batteries on the Georgia coast, Ulysses S. Grant and William T. Sherman were still schoolboys in Ohio, and Harriet Tubman was a ten-year-old field hand on a Maryland slave plantation. John Brown was teaching school and running a tannery in Pennsylvania, Stephen A. Douglas was reading law in western New York, Frederick Douglass was learning to read as an adolescent slave in Baltimore, and Harriet Beecher Stowe was teaching composition in her sister's Hartford Female Seminary. Their careers a generation hence would each be profoundly shaped and, in some cases, redirected by the process Garrison set in motion in 1831. With ferocious determination, Garrison broke the silence and made the public listen in a way that his predecessors had not. He employed a writing style of extraordinary physicality—in his columns trumpets blare, statues bleed, hearts melt, apologists tremble, light blazes, nations move—that animated the moral landscape as the Romantic poets had spiritualized the natural world, and he made the moral issue of slavery so palpable that it could no longer be evaded. "Surely, no man yet/ Put lever to the heavy world with less," the poet James Russell Lowell wrote in 1848. "What need of help?—He knew how types were set,/ He had a dauntless spirit and a press."

Nat Turner's Slave Rebellion

NAT TURNER

Nat Turner, a Virginia slave originally belonging to a family named Turner, was born in 1800. As a young man, Turner claimed to have had visitations from the Holy Spirit, who reportedly told Turner to "fight against the Serpent," whom Turner understood to be white slave masters. In August 1831, Turner recruited more than sixty fellow slaves to plan a slave rebellion in Southampton County, Virginia. On August 22, Turner launched his rebellion and led his followers on a killing spree that resulted in the deaths of about sixty white people. Turner was eventually captured, tried, found guilty, and executed for his actions. Before his execution, Turner narrated his story to an attorney, Thomas R. Gray, who published Turner's narrative as *The Confessions of Nat Turner*. This excerpt from that text reveals how Turner came to initiate his rebellion and how he carried out his murderous work.

As I was praying one day at my plough, the spirit spoke to me, saying "Seek ye the kingdom of Heaven and all things shall be added unto you.["]. . .

After this revelation in the year 1825, and the knowledge of the elements being made known to me, I sought more than ever to obtain true holiness before the great day of judgment should appear, and then I began to receive the true knowledge of faith. And from the first steps of righteousness until the last, was I made perfect; and the Holy Ghost was with me, and said, "Behold me as I stand in the Heavens"—and I looked and saw the forms of men in different attitudes—and there were lights in the sky to which the children of darkness gave other names than what they really were—for they were the lights of the Sav-

Kenneth S. Greenberg, ed., *The Confessions of Nat Turner and Related Documents*. Boston: Bedford Books of St. Martin's Press, 1996.

iour's hands, stretched forth from east to west, even as they were extended on the cross on Calvary for the redemption of sinners. And I wondered greatly at these miracles, and prayed to be informed of a certainty of the meaning thereof—and shortly afterwards, while laboring in the field, I discovered drops of blood on the corn as though it were dew from heaven—and I communicated it to many, both white and black, in the neighborhood—and I then found on the leaves in the woods hieroglyphic characters, and numbers, with the forms of men in different attitudes, portrayed in blood, and representing the figures I had seen before in the heavens. And now the Holy Ghost had revealed itself to me, and made plain the miracles it had shown me—For as the blood of Christ had been shed on this earth, and had ascended to heaven for the salvation of sinners, and was now returning to earth again in the form of dew—and as the leaves on the trees bore the impression of the figures I had seen in the heavens, it was plain to me that the Saviour was about to lay down the yoke he had borne for the sins of men, and the great day of judgement was at hand.

SIGNS FROM HEAVEN

About this time I told these things to a white man, (Etheldred T. Brantley) on whom it had a wonderful effect—and he ceased from his wickedness, and was attacked immediately with a cutaneous eruption, and blood oozed from the pores of his skin, and after praying and fasting nine days, he was healed, and the Spirit appeared to me again, and said, as the Saviour had been baptised so should we be also—and when the white people would not let us be baptised by the church, we went down into the water together, in the sight of many who reviled us, and were baptised by the Spirit—After this I rejoiced greatly, and gave thanks to God. And on the 12th of May, 1828, I heard a loud noise in the heavens, and the Spirit instantly appeared to me and said the Serpent was loosened, and Christ had laid down the yoke he had borne for the sins of men, and that I should take it on and fight against the Serpent, for the time was fast approaching when the first should be last and the last should be first. . . .

Since the commencement of 1830, I had been living with Mr. Joseph Travis, who was to me a kind master, and placed the greatest confidence in me; in fact, I had no cause to complain of his treatment to me. On Saturday evening, the 20th of August, it was agreed between Henry, Hark and myself, to prepare a dinner the next day for the men we expected, and then to concert a plan, as we had not yet determined on any. Hark, on the following morning, brought a pig, and Henry brandy, and being joined by Sam, Nelson, Will and Jack, they prepared in the woods a dinner, where about three o'clock, I joined them. . . .

THE REBELLION BEGINS

I saluted them on coming up, and asked Will how came he there, he answered, his life was worth no more than others, and his liberty as dear to him. I asked him if he thought to obtain it? He said he would, or lose his life. This was enough to put him in full confidence. Jack, I knew, was only a tool in the hands of Hark, it was quickly agreed we should commence at home (Mr. J. Travis') on that night, and until we had armed and equipped ourselves, and gathered sufficient force, neither age nor sex was to be spared, (which was invariably adhered to). We remained at the feast, until about two hours in the night, when we went to the house and found Austin; they all went to the cider press and drank, except myself. On returning to the house, Hark went to the door with an axe, for the purpose of breaking it open, as we knew we were strong enough to murder the family, if they were awaked by the noise; but reflecting that it might create an alarm in the neighborhood, we determined to enter the house secretly, and murder them whilst sleeping. Hark got a ladder and set it against the chimney, on which I ascended, and hoisting a window, entered and came down stairs, unbarred the door, and removed the guns from their places. It was then observed that I must spill the first blood. On which, armed with a hatchet, and accompanied by Will, I entered my master's chamber, it being dark, I could not give a death blow, the hatchet glanced from his head, he sprang from the bed and called his wife, it was his last word, Will laid him dead, with a blow of his axe, and Mrs. Travis shared the same fate, as she lay in bed. The murder of this family, five in number, was the work of a moment, not one of them awoke; there was a little infant sleeping in a cradle, that was forgotten, until we had left the house and gone some distance, when Henry and Will returned and killed it; we got here, four guns that would shoot, and several old muskets, with a pound or two of powder. We remained some time at the barn, where we paraded; I formed them in a line as soldiers, and after carrying them through all the manœvres I was master of, marched them off to Mr. Salathul Francis', about six hundred yards distant. Sam and Will went to the door and knocked. Mr. Francis asked who was there, Sam replied it was him, and he had a letter for him, on which he got up and came to the door; they immediately seized him, and dragging him out a little from the door, he was dispatched by repeated blows on the head; there was no other white person in the family. We started from there for Mrs. Reese's, maintaining the most perfect silence on our march, where finding the door unlocked, we entered, and murdered Mrs. Reese in her bed, while sleeping; her son awoke, but it was only to sleep the sleep of death, he had only time to say who is that, and he was no more.

A KILLING SPREE

From Mrs. Reese's we went to Mrs. Turner's, a mile distant, which we reached about sunrise, on Monday morning. Henry, Austin, and Sam, went to the still, where, finding Mr. Peebles, Austin shot him, and the rest of us went to the house; as we approached, the family discovered us, and shut the door. Vain hope! Will, with one stroke of his axe, opened it, and we entered and found Mrs. Turner and Mrs. Newsome in the middle of a room, almost frightened to death. Will immediately killed Mrs. Turner, with one blow of his axe. I took Mrs. Newsome by the hand, and with the sword I had when I was apprehended, I struck her several blows over the head, but not being able to kill her, as the sword was dull. Will turning around and discovering it, despatched her also. A general destruction of property and search for money and ammunition, always suc-

ceeded the murders. By this time my company amounted to fifteen, and nine men mounted, who started for Mrs. Whitehead's,
(the other six were to go through a by way to Mr. Bryant's, and
rejoin us at Mrs. Whitehead's,) as we approached the house we
discovered Mr. Richard Whitehead standing in the cotton
patch, near the lane fence; we called him over into the lane, and
Will, the executioner, was near at hand, with his fatal axe, to
send him to an untimely grave. As we pushed on to the house,
I discovered some one run round the garden, and thinking it
was some of the white family, I pursued them, but finding it
was a servant girl belonging to the house, I returned to commence the work of death, but they whom I left, had not been
idle; all the family were already murdered, but Mrs. Whitehead
and her daughter Margaret. As I came round to the door I saw
Will pulling Mrs. Whitehead out of the house, and at the step
he nearly severed her head from her body, with his broad axe.
Miss Margaret, when I discovered her, had concealed herself in
the corner, formed by the projection of the cellar cap from the
house; on my approach she fled, but was soon overtaken, and after repeated blows with a sword, I killed her by a blow on the
head, with a fence rail. By this time, the six who had gone by
Mr. Bryant's, rejoined us, and informed me they had done the
work of death assigned them. We again divided, part going to
Mr. Richard Porter's, and from thence to Nathaniel Francis',
the others to Mr. Howell Harris', and Mr. T. Doyles'. On my reaching Mr. Porter's, he had escaped with his family. I understood
there, that the alarm had already spread, and I immediately returned to bring up those sent to Mr. Doyles', and Mr. Howell
Harris'; the party I left going on to Mr. Francis', having told
them I would join them in that neighborhood. I met those sent
to Mr. Doyles' and Mr. Harris' returning, having met Mr. Doyle
on the road and killed him; and learning from some who joined
them, that Mr. Harris was from home, I immediately pursued
the course taken by the party gone on before; but knowing they
would complete the work of death and pillage, at Mr. Francis'
before I could get there, I went to Mr. Peter Edwards', expect-
ing to find them there, but they had been here also. I then went

In 1831 Nat Turner led an insurrection of slaves in Virginia. They killed approximately sixty white people before Turner was captured.

to Mr. John T. Barrow's, they had been here and murdered him. I pursued on their track to Capt. Newit Harris', where I found the greater part mounted, and ready to start; the men now amounting to about forty, shouted and hurraed as I rode up, some were in the yard, loading their guns, others drinking. They said Captain Harris and his family had escaped, the property in the house they destroyed, robbing him of money and other valuables. I ordered them to mount and march instantly, this was about nine or ten o'clock, Monday morning. I proceeded to Mr. Levi Waller's, two or three miles distant. I took my station in the rear, and as it 'twas my object to carry terror and devastation wherever we went, I placed fifteen or twenty of the best armed and most to be relied on, in front, who generally approached the house as fast as their horses could run; this was for two purposes, to prevent their escape and strike terror to the inhabitants—on this account I never got to the houses, after leaving Mrs. Whitehead's, until the murders were committed, except in one case. I sometimes got in sight in time to see the work of death completed, viewed the mangled bodies as they lay, in silent satisfaction, and immediately started in quest of other victims—Having murdered Mrs. Waller and ten children, we started for Mr. William Williams'—having killed him and two little boys that were there; while engaged in this, Mrs. Williams fled and got some distance from the house, but she was pursued, overtaken, and compelled to get up behind one of the company, who brought her back, and after showing her the mangled body of her lifeless husband, she was told to get down and lay by his side, where she was shot dead. I then started for Mr. Jacob Williams, where the family were murdered—Here we found a young man named Drury, who had come on business with Mr. Williams—he was pursued, overtaken and shot. Mrs. Vaughan was the next place we visited—and after murdering the family here, I determined on starting for Jerusalem.

THE REBELLION SPREADS

Our number amounted now to fifty or sixty, all mounted and armed with guns, axes, swords and clubs—On reaching Mr. James W. Parkers' gate, immediately on the road leading to Jerusalem, and about three miles distant, it was proposed to me to call there, but I objected, as I knew he was gone to Jerusalem, and my object was to reach there as soon as possible; but some of the men having relations at Mr. Parker's it was agreed that they might call and get his people. I remained at the gate on the road, with seven or eight; the others going across the field to the house, about half a mile off. After waiting some time for them, I became impatient, and started to the house for them, and on our return we were met by a party of white men, who had pursued our blood-stained track, and who had fired on those at the gate, and dispersed them, which I [k]new nothing of, not having been at that time rejoined by any of them—Immediately on discovering the whites, I ordered my men to halt and form, as they appeared to be alarmed—The white men, eighteen in number, approached us in about one hundred yards, when one of them fired, (this was against the positive orders of Captain Alexander P. Peete, who commanded, and who had directed the men to reserve their fire until within thirty paces). And I discovered about half of them retreating, I then ordered my men to fire and rush on them; the few remaining stood their ground until we approached within fifty yards, when they fired and retreated. We pursued and overtook some of them who we thought we left dead; (they were not killed) after pursuing them about two hundred yards, and rising a little hill, I discovered they were met by another party, and had haulted, and were reloading their guns, (this was a small party from Jerusalem who knew the negroes were in the field, and had just tied their horses to await their return to the road, knowing that Mr. Parker and family were in Jerusalem, but knew nothing of the party that had gone in with Captain Peete; on hearing the firing they immediately rushed to the spot and arrived just in time to arrest the progress of these barbarous villains, and save the lives of their friends and fellow citizens). Thinking that those who retreated first, and the party who fired on us at fifty or sixty yards distant, had all only fallen back to meet others with amunition.

As I saw them re-loading their guns, and more coming up than I saw at first, and several of my bravest men being wounded, the others became panick struck and squandered over the field; the white men pursued and fired on us several times. Hark had his horse shot under him, and I caught another for him as it was running by me; five or six of my men were wounded, but none left on the field; finding myself defeated here I instantly determined to go through a private way, and cross the Nottoway river at the Cypress Bridge, three miles below Jerusalem, and attack that place in the rear, as I expected they would look for me on the other road, and I had a great desire to get there to procure arms and amunition. After going a short distance in this private way, accompanied by about twenty men, I overtook two or three who told me the others were dispersed in every direction. After tyring [sic] in vain to collect a sufficient force to proceed to Jerusalem, I determined to return, as I was sure they would make back to their old neighborhood, where they would rejoin me, make new recruits, and come down again. On my way back, I called at Mrs. Thomas's, Mrs. Spencer's, and several other places, the white families having fled, we found no more victims to gratify our thirst for blood, we stopped at Majr. Ridley's quarter for the night, and being joined by four of his men, with the recruits made since my defeat, we mustered now about forty strong. After placing out sentinels, I laid down to sleep, but was quickly roused by a great racket; starting up, I found some mounted, and others in great confusion; one of the sentinels having given the alarm that we were about to be attacked, I ordered some to ride round and reconnoitre, and on their return the others being more alarmed, not knowing who they were, fled in different ways, so that I was reduced to about twenty again; with this I determined to attempt to recruit, and proceed on to rally in the neighborhood, I had left. Dr. Blunt's was the nearest house, which we reached just before day; on riding up the yard, Hark fired a gun. We expected Dr. Blunt and his family were at Maj. Ridley's, as I knew there was a company of men there; the gun was fired to ascertain if any of the family were at home; we were immediately fired upon and retreated, leaving several of my men. I do not know what became of them, as I never saw them afterwards. Pursuing our course back and coming in sight of Captain Harris', where we had been the day before, we discovered a party of white men at the house, on which all deserted me but two, (Jacob and Nat,) we concealed ourselves in the woods until near night, when I sent them in search of Henry, Sam, Nelson, and Hark, and directed them to rally all they could, at the place we had had our dinner the Sunday before, where they would find me, and I accordingly returned there as soon as it was dark and remained until Wednesday evening, when discovering white men riding around the place as though they were looking for some one, and none of my men joining me, I concluded Jacob and Nat had been taken, and compelled to betray me. On this

I gave up all hope for the present; and on Thursday night after having supplied myself with provisions from Mr. Travis's, I scratched a hole under a pile of fence rails in a field, where I concealed myself for six weeks, never leaving my hiding place but for a few minutes in the dead of night to get water which was very near; thinking by this time I could venture out, I began to go about in the night and eaves drop the houses in the neighborhood; pursuing this course for about a fortnight and gathering little or no intelligence, afraid of speaking to any human being, and returning every morning to my cave before the dawn of day.

CAPTURED

I know not how long I might have led this life, if accident had not betrayed me, a dog in the neighborhood passing by my hiding place one night while I was out, was attracted by some meat I had in my cave, and crawled in and stole it, and was coming out just as I returned. A few nights after, two negroes having started to go hunting with the same dog, and passed that way, the dog came again to the place, and having just gone out to walk about, discovered me and barked, on which thinking myself discovered, I spoke to them to beg concealment. On making myself known they fled from me. Knowing then they would betray me, I immediately left my hiding place, and was pursued almost incessantly until I was taken a fortnight afterwards by Mr. Benjamin Phipps, in a little hole I had dug out with my sword, for the purpose of concealment, under the top of a fallen tree. On Mr. Phipps' discovering the place of my concealment, he cocked his gun and aimed at me. I requested him not to shoot and I would give up, upon which he demanded my sword. I delivered it to him, and he brought me to prison. During the time I was pursued, I had many hair breadth escapes, which your time will not permit you to relate. I am here loaded with chains, and willing to suffer the fate that awaits me.

A Woman's Role in the Abolitionist Movement

ANGELINA GRIMKÉ

Angelina Grimké and her older sister Sarah grew up in a slave-holding family in South Carolina. As young women, however, the Grimké sisters came upon Quaker abolitionist writings and developed a distaste for slavery. Both sisters eventually became devout Quakers devoted to abolition and to women's rights. In 1836, Angelina wrote *Appeal to the Christian Women of the South*, which is excerpted here. In this pamphlet, Angelina tries to convince southern women to turn their backs on their slave heritage and work toward emancipation. During a time when women could not vote, run for political office, or join the antislavery clergy, Angelina encourages women to become active abolitionists—to read about slavery, pray over it, speak about it, and act against it. In 1838, Angelina Grimké married the abolitionist author Theodore D. Weld, and she helped him conduct research for his influential antislavery text *American Slavery as It Is*, which was published in 1839.

I have thus, I think, clearly proved to you seven propositions, viz.: First, that slavery is contrary to the declaration of our independence. Second, that it is contrary to the first charter of human rights given to Adam, and renewed to Noah. Third, that the fact of slavery having been the subject of prophecy, furnishes *no* excuse whatever to slavedealers. Fourth, that no such system existed under the patriarchal dispensation. Fifth, that *slavery never* existed under the Jewish dispensation; but so far otherwise, that every servant was placed under the *protection of law*, and care taken not only to prevent all *involuntary* servitude, but

Angelina Grimké, *Appeal to the Christian Women of the South*. New York: New York Anti-Slavery Society, 1836.

all *voluntary perpetual* bondage. Sixth, that slavery in America reduces a *man* to a *thing*, a "chattel personal," *robs him* of *all* his rights as a *human being*, fetters both his mind and body, and protects the *master* in the most unnatural and unreasonable power, whilst it *throws him out* of the protection of law. Seventh, that slavery is contrary to the example and precepts of our holy and merciful Redeemer, and of his apostles.

But perhaps you will be ready to query, why appeal to *women* on this subject? *We* do not make the laws which perpetuate slavery. *No* legislative power is vested in *us; we* can do nothing to overthrow the system, even if we wished to do so. To this I reply, I know you do not make the laws, but I also know that *you are the wives and mothers, the sisters and daughters of those who do;* and if you really suppose *you* can do nothing to overthrow slavery, you are greatly mistaken. You can do much in every way: four things I will name. 1st. You can read on this subject. 2d. You can pray over this subject. 3d. You can speak on this subject. 4th. You can *act* on this subject. I have not placed reading before praying because I regard it more important, but because, in order to pray aright, we must understand what we are praying for; it is only then we can "pray with the understanding and the spirit also."

WHAT WOMEN CAN DO

1. Read then on the subject of slavery. Search the Scriptures daily, whether the things I have told you are true. Other books and papers might be a great help to you in this investigation, but they are not necessary, and it is hardly probable that your Committees of Vigilance will allow you to have any other. The *Bible* then is the book I want you to read in the spirit of inquiry, and the spirit of prayer. Even the enemies of Abolitionists, acknowledge that their doctrines are drawn from it. In the great mob in Boston last autumn, when the books and papers of the Anti-Slavery Society were thrown out of the windows of their office, an individual laid hold of the Bible and was about tossing it out to the ground, when another reminded him that it was the Bible he had in his hand. "*O! 'tis all one,*" he replied, and

out went the sacred volume along with the rest. We thank him for the acknowledgment. Yes, *"it is all one,"* for our books and papers are mostly commentaries on the Bible, and the Declaration. Read the *Bible* then, it contains the words of Jesus, and they are spirit and life. Judge for yourselves whether *he sanctioned* such a system of oppression and crime.

2. Pray over this subject. When you have entered into your closets, and shut to the doors, then pray to your father, who seeth in secret, that he would open your eyes to see whether slavery is *sinful*, and if it is, that he would enable you to bear a faithful, open and unshrinking testimony against it, and to do whatsoever your hands find to do, leaving the consequences entirely to him, who still says to us whenever we try to reason away duty from the fear of consequences, *"What is that to thee, follow thou me."* Pray also for that poor slave, that he may be kept patient and submissive under his hard lot, until God is pleased to open the door of freedom to him without violence or bloodshed. Pray too for the master that his heart may be softened, and he made willing to acknowledge, as Joseph's brethren did, "Verily we are guilty concerning our brother," before he will be compelled to add in consequence of Divine judgment, "therefore is all this evil come upon us." Pray also for all your brethren and sisters who are laboring in the righteous cause of Emancipation in the Northern States, England and the world. There is great encouragement for prayer in these words of our Lord. "Whatsoever ye shall ask the Father *in my name*, he *will give* it to you"—Pray then without ceasing, in the closet and the social circle.

3. Speak on this subject. It is through the tongue, the pen, and the press, that truth is principally propagated. Speak then to your relatives, your friends, your acquaintances on the subject of slavery; be not afraid if you are conscientiously convinced it is *sinful*, to say so openly, but calmly, and to let your sentiments be known. If you are served by the slaves of others, try to ameliorate their condition as much as possible; never aggravate their faults, and thus add fuel to the fire of anger already kindled in a master and mistress's bosom; remember their extreme igno-

rance, and consider them as your Heavenly Father does the *less* culpable on this account, even when they do wrong things. Discountenance *all* cruelty to them, all starvation, all corporal chastisement; these may brutalize and *break* their spirits, but will never bond them to willing, cheerful obedience. If possible, see that they are comfortably and *seasonably* fed, whether in the house or the field; it is unreasonable and cruel to expect slaves to wait for their breakfast until eleven o'clock, when they rise at five or six. Do all you can, to induce their owners to clothe them well, and to allow them many little indulgences which would contribute to their comfort. Above all, try to persuade your husband, father, brothers and sons, that *slavery is a crime against God and man*, and that it is a great sin to keep *human beings* in such abject ignorance; to deny them the privilege of learning to read and write. The Catholics are universally condemned, for denying the Bible to the common people, but, *slaveholders must not* blame them, for *they* are doing the *very same thing*, and for the very same reason, neither of these systems can bear the light which bursts from the pages of that Holy Book. And lastly, endeavour to inculcate submission on the part of the slaves, but whilst doing this be faithful in pleading the cause of the oppressed.

> Will *you* behold unheeding,
>   Life's holiest feelings crushed,
> Where *woman's* heart is bleeding,
>   Shall *woman's* heart be hushed?

4. Act on this subject. Some of you *own* slaves yourselves. If you believe slavery is *Sinful,* set them at liberty, "undo the heavy burdens and let the oppressed go free." If they wish to remain with you, pay them wages, if not let them leave you. Should they remain teach them, and have them taught the common branches of an English education; they have minds and those minds, *ought to be improved.* So precious a talent as intellect, never was given to be wrapt in a napkin and buried in the earth. It is the *duty* of all, as far as they can, to improve their own mental faculties, because we are commanded to love God with *all our*

minds, as well as with all our hearts, and we commit a great sin, if we *forbid or prevent* that cultivation of the mind in others, which would enable them to perform this duty. Teach your servants then to read &c, and encourage them to believe it is their *duty* to learn, if it were only that they might read the Bible. . . .

WOMEN ARE WORKING FOR EMANCIPATION

And what, I would ask in conclusion, have *women* done for the great and glorious cause of Emancipation? Who wrote that pamphlet which moved the heart of Wilberforce to pray over the wrongs, and his tongue to plead the cause of the oppressed African? It was a *woman*, Elizabeth Heyrick. Who labored assiduously to keep the sufferings of the slave continually before the British public? They were *women*. And how did they do it? By their needles, paint brushes and pens, by speaking the truth, and petitioning Parliament for the abolition of slavery. And what was the effect of their labors? Read it in the Emancipation bill of Great Britain. Read it, in the present state of her West India Colonies. Read it, in the impulse which has been given to the cause of freedom in the United States of America. Have English women then done so much for the negro, and shall American women do nothing? Oh no! Already are there sixty female Anti-Slavery Societies in operation. These are doing just what the English women did, telling the story of the colored man's wrongs, praying for his deliverance, and presenting his kneeling image constantly before the public eye on bags and needle-books, card-racks, pen-wipers, pin-cushions, &c. Even the children of the north are inscribing on their handy work, "May the points of our needles prick the slaveholder's conscience." Some of the reports of these Societies exhibit not only considerable talent, but a deep sense of religious duty, and a determination to persevere through evil as well as good report, until every scourge, and every shackle, is buried under the feet of the manumitted slave.

The Ladies' Anti-Slavery Society of Boston was called last fall, to a severe trial of their faith and constancy. They were mobbed by "the gentlemen of property and standing," in that city at their anniversary meeting, and their lives were jeoparded by an infuriated crowd; but their conduct on that occasion did credit to our sex, and affords a full assurance that they will *never* abandon the cause of the slave. The pamphlet, Right and Wrong in Boston, issued by them in which a particular account is given of that "mob of broad cloth in broad day," does equal credit to the head and the heart of her who wrote it. I wish my Southern sisters could read it; they would then understand that the women of the North have engaged in this work from a sense of *religious duty*, and that nothing will ever induce them to take their hands from it until it is fully accomplished. . . .

But why, my dear friends, have I thus been endeavoring to lead you through the history of more than three thousand years, and to point you to that great cloud of witnesses who have gone before, "from works to rewards"? Have I been seeking to magnify the sufferings, and exalt the character of woman, that she "might have praise of men"? No! no! my object has been to arouse *you*, as the wives and mothers, the daughters and sisters, of the South, to a sense of your duty as *women*, and as Christian women, on that great subject, which has already shaken our country, from the St. Lawrence and the lakes, to the Gulf of Mexico, and from the Mississippi to the shores of the Atlantic; *and will continue mightily to shake it*, until the polluted temple of slavery fall and crumble into ruin. . . .

The *women of the South can overthrow* this horrible system of oppression and cruelty, licentiousness and wrong. Such appeals to your legislatures would be irresistible, for there is something in the heart of man which *will bend under moral suasion*. There is a swift witness for truth in his bosom, which *will respond to truth* when it is uttered with calmness and dignity. If you could obtain but six signatures to such a petition in only one state, I would say, send up that petition, and be not in the least discouraged by the scoffs and jeers of the heartless, or the resolution of the house to lay it on the table. It will be a great thing if the subject can be introduced into your legislatures in any way, even by *women*, and *they* will be the most likely to introduce it there in the best possible manner, as a matter of *morals* and *religion*, not of expediency or politics. You may petition, too, the different ecclesiastical bodies of the slave states. Slavery must be attacked with the whole power of truth and the sword of the spirit. You must take it up on *Christian* ground, and fight against it with Christian weapons, whilst your feet are shod with the preparation of the gospel of peace. And *you are now* loudly called upon by the cries of the widow and the orphan, to arise and gird yourselves for this great moral conflict, with the whole armour of righteousness upon the right hand and on the left.

Slaves Must Agitate to Gain Their Freedom

HENRY HIGHLAND GARNET

Henry Highland Garnet was born a slave on a Maryland plantation in 1815. When he was still a child, his family escaped from slavery and settled in New York City. Garnet grew up in a household that was fiercely antislavery and devoutly religious. Garnet became a minister and railed against slavery from the pulpit and at antislavery meetings and conventions. Garnet delivered the following speech at the National Negro Convention in Buffalo in 1843. The speech identifies the evils of slavery and urges slaves to revolt against their masters. Speeches like this one marked Garnet as a radical abolitionist who advocated direct action, rather than prayer and moral suasion, to uproot slavery in the United States. Garnet predicted that blood might have to be shed to abolish American slavery. During the Civil War, Garnet became one of the first African American abolitionist leaders to encourage President Abraham Lincoln to allow African Americans to join the Union army.

B rethren and Fellow Citizens: Your brethren of the North, East, and West have been accustomed to meet together in National Conventions, to sympathize with each other, and to weep over your unhappy condition. In these meetings we have addressed all classes of the free, but we have never, until this time, sent a word of consolation and advice to you. We have been contented in sitting still and mourning over your sorrows, earnestly hoping that before this day your sacred liberties would have been restored. But, we have hoped in vain. Years have rolled on, and tens of thousands have been borne on streams of blood and tears to the shores of eternity. While you have been

Henry Highland Garnet, speech at the National Negro Convention, Buffalo, New York, 1843.

oppressed, we have also been partakers with you; nor can we be free while you are enslaved. We, therefore, write to you as being bound with you.

Many of you are bound to us, not only by the ties of a common humanity, but we are connected by the more tender relations of parents, wives, husbands, and sisters, and friends. As such we most affectionately address you.

Slavery has fixed a deep gulf between you and us, and while it shuts out from you the relief and consolation which your friends would willingly render, it afflicts and persecutes you with a fierceness which we might not expect to see in the fiends of hell. But still the Almighty Father of mercies has left to us a glimmering ray of hope, which shines out like a lone star in a cloudy sky. Mankind are becoming wiser, and better—the oppressor's power is fading, and you, every day, are becoming better informed, and more numerous. Your grievances, brethren, are many. We shall not attempt, in this short address, to present to the world all the dark catalogue of the nation's sins, which have been committed upon an innocent people. Nor is it indeed necessary, for you feel them from day to day, and all the civilized world looks upon them with amazement.

Two Centuries of Suffering

Two hundred and twenty-seven years ago the first of our injured race were brought to the shores of America. They came not with glad spirits to select their homes in the New World. They came not with their own consent, to find an unmolested enjoyment of the blessings of this fruitful soil. The first dealings they had with men calling themselves Christians exhibited to them the worst features of corrupt and sordid hearts: and convinced them that no cruelty is too great, no villainy and no robbery too abhorrent for even enlightened men to perform, when influenced by avarice and lust. Neither did they come flying upon the wings of liberty to a land of freedom. But they came with broken hearts, from their beloved native land, and were doomed to unrequited toil and deep degradation. Nor did the evil of their bondage end at their emancipation by death.

Succeeding generations inherited their chains, and millions have come from eternity into time, and have returned again to the world of spirits, cursed and ruined by American slavery.

The propagators of the system, or their immediate successors, very soon discovered its growing evil, and its tremendous wickedness, and secret promises were made to destroy it. The gross inconsistency of a people holding slaves, who had themselves "ferried o'er the wave" for freedom's sake, was too apparent to be entirely overlooked. The voice of Freedom cried, "Emancipate your slaves." Humanity supplicated with tears for the deliverance of the children of Africa. Wisdom urged her solemn plea. The bleeding captive plead his innocence, and pointed to Christianity who stood weeping at the cross. Jehovah frowned upon the nefarious institution, and thunderbolts, red with vengeance, struggled to leap forth to blast the guilty wretches who maintained it. But all was vain. Slavery had stretched its dark wings of death over the land, the Church stood silently by—the priests prophesied falsely, and the people loved to have it so. Its throne is established, and now it reigns triumphant.

Nearly three millions of your fellow-citizens are prohibited by law and public opinion (which in this country is stronger than law) from reading the Book of Life. Your intellect has been destroyed as much as possible, and every ray of light they have attempted to shut out from your minds. The oppressors themselves have become involved in the ruin. They have become weak, sensual, and rapacious—they have cursed you—they have cursed themselves—they have cursed the earth which they have trod.

The colonies threw the blame upon England. They said that the mother country entailed the evil upon them, and they would rid themselves of it if they could. The world thought they were sincere, and the philanthropic pitied them. But time soon tested their sincerity. In a few years the colonists grew strong, and severed themselves from the British Government. Their independence was declared, and they took their station among the sovereign powers of the earth. The declaration was a glorious document. Sages admired it, and the patriotic of every nation reverenced the God-like sentiments which it contained. When the power of Government returned to their hands, did they emancipate the slaves? No; they rather added new links to our chains. Were they ignorant of the principles of Liberty? Certainly they were not. The sentiments of their revolutionary orators fell in burning eloquence upon their hearts, and with one voice they cried, LIBERTY OR DEATH. Oh, what a sentence was that! It ran from soul to soul like electric fire, and nerved the arms of thousands to fight in the holy cause of Freedom. Among the diversity of opinions that are entertained in regard to physical resistance, there are but a few found to gainsay the stern declaration. We are among those who do not.

SLAVERY VIOLATES GOD'S COMMANDS

SLAVERY! How much misery is comprehended in that single word. What mind is there that does not shrink from its direful effects? Unless the image of God be obliterated from the soul, all men cherish the love of liberty. The nice discerning political economist does not regard the sacred right more than the untutored African who roams in the wilds of Congo. Nor has the one more right to the full enjoyment of his freedom than the other. In every man's mind the good seeds of liberty are planted, and he who brings his fellow down so low, as to make him contented with a condition of slavery, commits the highest crime against God and man. Brethren, your oppressors aim to do this. They endeavor to make you as much like brutes as possible. When they have blinded the eyes of your mind—when they have embittered the sweet waters of life—when they have shut out the light which shines from the word of God—then, and not till then, has American slavery done its perfect work.

TO SUCH DEGRADATION IT IS SINFUL IN THE EXTREME FOR YOU TO MAKE VOLUNTARY SUBMISSION. The divine commandments you are in duty bound to reverence and obey. If you do not obey them, you will surely meet with the displeasure of the Almighty. He requires you to love Him supremely, and your neighbor as yourself—to keep the Sabbath day holy—to search the Scriptures—and bring up your children with respect for His laws, and to worship no other God but Him. But slavery sets all these at nought, and hurls defiance in the face of Jehovah. The forlorn condition in which you are placed does not destroy your obligation to God. You are not certain of heaven, because you allow yourselves to remain in a state of slavery, where you cannot obey the commandments of the Sovereign of the universe. If the ignorance of slavery is a passport to heaven, then it is a

John Brown to the Court

In November 1859, John Brown was found guilty of starting a slave insurrection in Harpers Ferry, Virginia, and sentenced to die. His actions and subsequent trial brought new energy to the abolitionist movement. Below is an excerpt from his final statement to the court before sentencing.

This court acknowledges, as I suppose, the validity of the law of God. I see a book kissed here which I suppose to be the Bible, or at least the New Testament. That teaches me that all things whatsoever I would that men should do to me, I should do even so to them. It teaches me, further, to "remember them that are in bonds, as bound with them." I endeavored to act up to that instruction. . . . I believe that to have interfered as I have done—as I have always freely admitted I have done—in behalf of His despised poor, was not wrong, but right. Now, if it is deemed necessary that I should forfeit my life for the furtherance of the ends of justice, and mingle my blood further with the blood of my children and with the blood of millions in this slave country whose rights are disregarded by wicked, cruel, and unjust enactments,—I submit; so let it be done!

Louis Ruchames, ed., *A John Brown Reader*. London: Abelard-Schuman, 1959.

blessing, and no curse, and you should rather desire its perpetuity than its abolition. God will not receive slavery, nor ignorance, nor any other state of mind, for love and obedience to Him. Your condition does not absolve you from your moral obligation. The diabolical injustice by which your liberties are cloven down, NEITHER GOD NOR ANGELS, OR JUST MEN, COMMAND YOU TO SUFFER FOR A SINGLE MOMENT. THEREFORE IT IS YOUR SOLEMN AND IMPERATIVE DUTY TO USE EVERY MEANS, BOTH MORAL, INTELLECTUAL, AND PHYSICAL, THAT PROMISES SUCCESS. If a band of heathen men should attempt to enslave a race of Christians, and to place their children under the influence of some false religion, surely Heaven would frown upon the men who would not resist such aggression, even to death. If, on the other hand, a band of Christians should attempt to enslave a race of heathen men, and to entail slavery upon them, and to keep them in heathenism in the midst of Christianity, the God of heaven would smile upon every effort which the injured might make to disenthral themselves.

Brethren, it is as wrong for your lordly oppressors to keep you in slavery as it was for the man thief to steal our ancestors from the coast of Africa. You should therefore now use the same manner of resistance as would have been just in our ancestors when the bloody foot-prints of the first remorseless soul-thief was placed upon the shores of our fatherland. The humblest peasant is as free in the sight of God as the proudest monarch that ever swayed a sceptre. Liberty is a spirit sent out from God, and like its great Author, is no respecter of persons.

A TIME FOR ACTION

Brethren, the time has come when you must act for yourselves. It is an old and true saying that, "if hereditary bondmen would be free, they must themselves strike the blow." You can plead your own cause, and do the work of emancipation better than any others. The nations of the Old World are moving in the great cause of universal freedom, and some of them at least will, ere long, do you justice. The combined powers of Europe have placed their broad seal of disapprobation upon the African slave-trade. But in the slaveholding parts of the United States the trade is as brisk as ever. They buy and sell you as though you were brute beasts. The North has done much—her opinion of slavery in the abstract is known. But in regard to the South, we adopt the opinion of the *New York Evangelist*—"We have advanced so far, that the cause apparently waits for a more effectual door to be thrown open than has been yet." We are about to point you to that more effectual door. Look around you, and behold the bosoms of your loving wives heaving with untold agonies! Here [*sic*] the cries of your poor children! Remember the stripes your fathers bore. Think of the torture and disgrace of your noble mothers. Think of your wretched sisters, loving virtue and purity, as they are driven into concubinage and are exposed to the unbridled lusts of incarnate devils. Think of the undying glory that hangs around the ancient name of Africa—and forget not that you are native-born American citizens, and as such you are justly entitled to all the rights that are granted to the freest. Think how many tears you have poured out upon the soil which you have cultivated with unrequited toil and enriched with your blood; and then go to your lordly enslavers and tell them plainly, that you *are determined to be free.* Appeal to their sense of justice, and tell them that they have no more right to oppress you than you have to enslave them. Entreat them to remove the grievous burdens which they have imposed upon you, and to remunerate you for your labor. Promise them renewed diligence in the cultivation of the soil, if they will render to you an equivalent for your services. Point them to the increase of happiness and prosperity in the British West Indies since the Act of Emancipation. Tell them in language which they cannot misunderstand of the exceeding sinfulness of slavery, and of a future judgment, and of the righteous retributions of an indignant God. Inform them that all you desire is FREE-DOM, and that nothing else will suffice. Do this, and forever after cease to toil for the heartless tyrants, who give you no other reward but stripes and abuse. If they then commence [the] work of death, they, and not you, will be responsible for the consequences. You had far better all die—*die immediately*, than live slaves, and entail your wretchedness upon your posterity. If you would be free in this generation, here is your only hope. However much you and all of us may desire it, there is not much hope of redemption without the shedding of blood. If you must bleed, let it all come at once—rather *die freemen than live to be the slaves*. It is impossible, like the children of Israel, to make a grand exodus from the land of bondage. The Pharaohs are on both sides of the blood-red waters! You cannot move *en masse* to the dominions of the British Queen—nor can you pass through Florida and overrun Texas, and at last find peace in Mexico. The propagators of American slavery are spending their blood and treasure that they may plant the black flag in the heart of Mexico and riot in the halls of the Montezumas. In language of the reverend Robert Hall, when addressing the volunteers of Bristol, who were rushing forth to repel the invasion of Napoleon, who threatened to lay waste the fair homes of England, "Religion is too much interested in your behalf not to shed over you her most gracious influences."

You will not be compelled to spend much time in order to become inured to hardships. From the first movement that you breathed the air of heaven, you have been accustomed to nothing else but hardships. The heroes of the American Revolution were never put upon harder fare than a peck of corn and [a] few herrings per week. You have not become enervated by the luxuries of life. Your sternest energies have been beaten out upon the anvil of severe trial. Slavery has done more than this, it has prepared you for any emergency. If you receive good treatment, it is what you can hardly expect; if you meet with pain, sorrow, and even death, these are the common lot of the slaves.

LIBERTY OR DEATH

Fellowmen! patient sufferers! behold your dearest rights crushed to the earth! See your sons murdered, and your wives, mothers and sisters doomed to prostitution. In the name of the merciful God, and by all that life is worth, let it no longer be a debatable question, whether it is better to choose *liberty* or *death*.

In 1822, Denmark Veazie, of South Carolina, formed a plan

for the liberation of his fellowmen. In the whole history of human efforts to overthrow slavery, a more complicated and tremendous plan was never formed. He was betrayed by the treachery of his own people, and died a martyr to freedom. Many a brave hero fell, but history, faithful to her high trust, will transcribe his name on the same monument with Moses, [John] Hampden, [William] Tell, [King Robert the] Bruce and [Sir William] Wallace, Toussaint L'Ouverture, [Marquis de] Lafayette, and [George] Washington. That tremendous movement shook the whole empire of slavery. The guilty soul-thieves were overwhelmed with fear. It is a matter of fact that at this time, and in consequence of the threatened revolution, the slave States talked strongly of emancipation. But they blew but one blast of the trumpet of freedom, and then laid it aside. As these men became quiet, the slaveholders ceased to talk about emancipation: and now behold your condition to-day! Angels sigh over it, and humanity has long since exhausted her tears in weeping on your account!

The patriotic Nathaniel Turner followed Denmark Veazie. He was goaded to desperation by wrong and injustice. By despotism, his name has been recorded on the list of infamy, and future generations will remember him among the noble and brave.

Next arose the immortal Joseph Cinque, the hero of the *Amistad*. He was a native African, and by the help of God he emancipated a whole shipload of his fellowmen on the high seas. And he now sings of liberty on the sunny hills of Africa and beneath his native palm-trees, where he hears the lion roar and feels himself as free as the king of the forest.

Next arose Madison Washington, that bright star of freedom, and took his station in the constellation of true heroism. He was a slave on board the brig *Creole*, of Richmond, bound to New Orleans, that great slave mart, with a hundred and four others. Nineteen struck for liberty or death. But one life was taken, and the whole were emancipated, and the vessel was carried into Nassau, New Providence.

Noble men! Those who have fallen in freedom's conflict, their memories will be cherished by the true-hearted and the

God-fearing in all future generations; those who are living, their names are surrounded by a halo of glory.

STRIKE THE OPPRESSORS

Brethren, arise, arise! Strike for your lives and liberties. Now is the day and the hour. Let every slave throughout the land do this, and the days of slavery are numbered. You cannot be more oppressed than you have been—you cannot suffer greater cruelties than you have already. *Rather die freemen than live to be slaves.* Remember that you are FOUR MILLIONS!

It is in your power so to torment the God-cursed slaveholders that they will be glad to let you go free. If the scale was turned, and black men were the masters and white men the slaves, every destructive agent and element would be employed to lay the oppressor low. Danger and death would hang over their heads day and night. Yes, the tyrants would meet with plagues more terrible than those of Pharaoh. But you are a patient people. You act as though you were made for the special use of these devils. You act as though your daughters were born to pamper the lusts of your masters and overseers. And worse than all, you tamely submit while your lords tear your wives from your embraces and defile them before your eyes. In the name of God, we ask, are you men? Where is the blood of your fathers? Has it all run out of your veins? Awake, awake; millions of voices are calling you! Your dead fathers speak to you from their graves. Heaven, as with a voice of thunder, calls on you to arise from the dust.

Let your motto be resistance! *resistance!* RESISTANCE! No oppressed people have ever secured their liberty without resistance. What kind of resistance you had better make you must decide by the circumstances that surround you, and according to the suggestion of expediency. Brethren, adieu! Trust in the living God. Labor for the peace of the human race, and remember that you are FOUR MILLIONS!

A Sermon on Slavery

HARRIET BEECHER STOWE

Harriet Beecher Stowe was born into a New England abolitionist family in 1811. Despite her family's leanings, she remained relatively inactive in the abolitionist movement until 1850. After the passage of the Fugitive Slave Law, which was part of the Compromise of 1850, Stowe decided to take some direct action against slavery. In 1851, she began to write a series of sketches about a fictional slave named Uncle Tom for the *National Era*, a weekly abolitionist newspaper. Readers became obsessed with the story, and Stowe contracted to have her tale of Uncle Tom published as a novel. *Uncle Tom's Cabin* became a runaway bestseller—and the single most effective piece of antislavery literature. The novel, which became popular in Europe as well, turned Stowe into an international celebrity. Stowe, whose father, brother, and husband were influential clergymen, concluded *Uncle Tom's Cabin* with a sermon against slavery, predicting that God would one day take vengeance upon the nation for the sin of slavery.

For many years of her life, the author avoided all reading upon or allusion to the subject of slavery, considering it as too painful to be inquired into, and one which advancing light and civilization would certainly live down. But, since the legislative act of 1850, when she heard, with perfect surprise and consternation, Christian and humane people actually recommending the remanding escaped fugitives into slavery, as a duty binding on good citizens,—when she heard, on all hands, from kind, compassionate and estimable people, in the free states of the North, deliberations and discussions as to what Christian duty could be on this head,—she could only think, These men and Christians cannot know what slavery is; if they did, such a

Harriet Beecher Stowe, *Uncle Tom's Cabin*, 1851.

question could never be open for discussion. And from this arose a desire to exhibit it in a *living dramatic reality*. She has endeavored to show it fairly, in its best and its worst phases. In its *best* aspect, she has, perhaps, been successful; but, oh! who shall say what yet remains untold in that valley and shadow of death, that lies the other side?

SLAVERY BREEDS DESPOTS

To you, generous, noble-minded men and women, of the South,—you, whose virtue, and magnanimity, and purity of character, are the greater for the severer trial it has encountered,—to you is her appeal. Have you not, in your own secret souls, in your own private conversings, felt that there are woes and evils, in this accursed system, far beyond what are here shadowed, or can be shadowed? Can it be otherwise? Is *man* ever a creature to be trusted with wholly irresponsible power? And does not the slave system, by denying the slave all legal right of testimony, make every individual owner an irresponsible despot? Can anybody fail to make the inference what the practical result will be? If there is, as we admit, a public sentiment among you, men of honor, justice and humanity, is there not also another kind of public sentiment among the ruffian, the brutal and debased? And cannot the ruffian, the brutal, the debased, by slave law, own just as many slaves as the best and purest? Are the honorable, the just, the high-minded and compassionate, the majority anywhere in this world?

The slave-trade is now, by American law, considered as piracy. But a slave-trade, as systematic as ever was carried on on the coast of Africa, is an inevitable attendant and result of American slavery. And its heartbreak and its horrors, *can* they be told?

The writer has given only a faint shadow, a dim picture, of the anguish and despair that are, at this very moment, riving thousands of hearts, shattering thousands of families, and driving a helpless and sensitive race to frenzy and despair. There are those living who know the mothers whom this accursed traffic has driven to the murder of their children; and themselves seeking in death a shelter from woes more dreaded than death.

Nothing of tragedy can be written, can be spoken, can be conceived, that equals the frightful reality of scenes daily and hourly acting on our shores, beneath the shadow of American law, and the shadow of the cross of Christ.

A CALL TO THE PEOPLE OF THE FREE STATES

And now, men and women of America, is this a thing to be trifled with, apologized for, and passed over in silence? Farmers of Massachusetts, of New Hampshire, of Vermont, of Connecticut, who read this book by the blaze of your winter-evening fire,—strong-hearted, generous sailors and ship-owners of Maine,—is this a thing for you to countenance and encourage? Brave and generous men of New York, farmers of rich and joyous Ohio, and ye of the wide prairie states,—answer, is this a thing for you to protect and countenance? And you, mothers of America,—you, who have learned, by the cradles of your own children, to love and feel for all mankind,—by the sacred love you bear your child; by your joy in his beautiful, spotless infancy; by the motherly pity and tenderness with which you guide his growing years; by the anxieties of his education; by the prayers you breathe for his soul's eternal good;—I beseech you, pity the mother who has all your affections, and not one legal right to protect, guide, or educate, the child of her bosom! By the sick hour of your child; by those dying eyes, which you can never forget; by those last cries, that wrung your heart when you could neither help nor save; by the desolation of that empty cradle, that silent nursery,—I beseech you, pity those mothers that are constantly made childless by the American slave-trade! And say, mothers of America, is this a thing to be defended, sympathized with, passed over in silence?

Do you say that the people of the free states have nothing to do with it, and can do nothing? Would to God this were true! But it is not true. The people of the free states have defended, encouraged, and participated; and are more guilty for it, before God, than the South, in that they have *not* the apology of education or custom.

If the mothers of the free states had all felt as they should, in times past, the sons of the free states would not have been the holders, and, proverbially, the hardest masters of slaves; the sons of the free states would not have connived at the extension of slavery, in our national body; the sons of the free states would not, as they do, trade the souls and bodies of men as an equivalent to money, in their mercantile dealings. There are multitudes of slaves temporarily owned, and sold again, by merchants in northern cities; and shall the whole guilt or obloquy of slavery fall only on the South?

Northern men, northern mothers, northern Christians, have something more to do than denounce their brethren at the South; they have to look to the evil among themselves. But, what can any individual do? Of that, every individual can judge. There is one thing that every individual can do,—they can see to it that *they feel right*. An atmosphere of sympathetic influence encircles every human being; and the man or woman who *feels* strongly, healthily and justly, on the great interests of humanity, is a constant benefactor to the human race. See, then, to your sympathies in this matter! Are they in harmony with the sympathies of Christ? or are they swayed and perverted by the sophistries of worldly policy?

Christian men and women of the North! still further,—you have another power; you can *pray!* Do you believe in prayer? or has it become an indistinct apostolic tradition? You pray for the heathen abroad; pray also for the heathen at home. And pray for those distressed Christians whose whole chance of religious improvement is an accident of trade and sale; from whom any adherence to the morals of Christianity is, in many cases, an impossibility, unless they have given them, from above, the courage and grace of martyrdom.

But, still more. On the shores of our free states are emerging the poor, shattered, broken remnants of families,—men and women, escaped, by miraculous providences, from the surges of slavery,—feeble in knowledge, and, in many cases, infirm in moral constitution, from a system which confounds and confuses every principle of Christianity and morality. They come to seek a refuge among you; they come to seek education, knowledge, Christianity.

A Home in Africa for Freed Slaves?

What do you owe to these poor unfortunates, oh Christians? Does not every American Christian owe to the African race some effort at reparation for the wrongs that the American nation has brought upon them? Shall the doors of churches and school-houses be shut upon them? Shall states arise and shake them out? Shall the church of Christ hear in silence the taunt that is thrown at them, and shrink away from the helpless hand that they stretch out; and, by her silence, encourage the cruelty that would chase them from our borders? If it must be so, it will be a mournful spectacle. If it must be so, the country will have reason to tremble, when it remembers that the fate of nations is in the hands of One who is very pitiful, and of tender compassion.

Do you say, "We don't want them here; let them go to Africa"?

That the providence of God has provided a refuge in Africa, is, indeed, a great and noticeable fact; but that is no reason why the church of Christ should throw off that responsibility to this outcast race which her profession demands of her.

To fill up Liberia with an ignorant, inexperienced, half-barbarized race, just escaped from the chains of slavery, would be only to prolong, for ages, the period of struggle and conflict which attends the inception of new enterprises. Let the church of the north receive these poor sufferers in the spirit of Christ; receive them to the educating advantages of Christian republican society and schools, until they have attained to somewhat of a moral and intellectual maturity, and then assist them in their passage to those shores, where they may put in practice the lessons they have learned in America.

The Need for Education

There is a body of men at the north, comparatively small, who have been doing this; and, as the result, this country has already seen examples of men, formerly slaves, who have rapidly acquired property, reputation, and education. Talent has been developed, which, considering the circumstances, is certainly remarkable; and, for moral traits of honesty, kindness, tenderness of feeling,—for heroic efforts and self-denials, endured for the ransom of brethren and friends yet in slavery,—they have been remarkable to a degree that, considering the influence under which they were born, is surprising.

Harriet Beecher Stowe

The writer has lived, for many years, on the frontier-line of slave states, and has had great opportunities of observation among those who formerly were slaves. They have been in her family as servants; and, in default of any other school to receive them, she has, in many cases, had them instructed in a family school, with her own children. She has also the testimony of missionaries, among the fugitives in Canada, in coincidence with her own experience; and her deductions, with regard to the capabilities of the race, are encouraging in the highest degree.

The first desire of the emancipated slave, generally, is for *education*. There is nothing that they are not willing to give or do to have their children instructed; and, so far as the writer has observed herself, or taken the testimony of teachers among them, they are remarkably intelligent and quick to learn. The results of schools, founded for them by benevolent individuals in Cincinnati, fully establish this. . . .

SLAVES EXHIBIT SELF-RELIANCE

The writer well remembers an aged colored woman, who was employed as a washerwoman in her father's family. The daughter of this woman married a slave. She was a remarkably active and capable young woman, and, by her industry and thrift, and the most persevering self-denial, raised nine hundred dollars for her husband's freedom, which she paid, as she raised it, into the hands of his master. She yet wanted a hundred dollars of the price, when he died. She never recovered any of the money.

These are but few facts, among multitudes which might be adduced, to show the self-denial, energy, patience, and honesty, which the slave has exhibited in a state of freedom.

And let it be remembered that these individuals have thus bravely succeeded in conquering for themselves comparative wealth and social position, in the face of every disadvantage and discouragement. The colored man, by the law of Ohio, cannot be a voter, and, till within a few years, was even denied the right of testimony in legal suits with the white. Nor are these instances confined to the State of Ohio. In all states of the Union we see men, but yesterday burst from the shackles of slavery, who, by a self-educating force, which cannot be too much admired, have risen to highly respectable stations in society. [J.W.C.] Pennington, among clergymen, [Frederick] Douglas and [Samuel Ringgold] Ward, among editors, are well known instances.

If this persecuted race, with every discouragement and disadvantage, have done thus much, how much more they might do, if the Christian church would act towards them in the spirit of her Lord?

A DAY OF RECKONING WILL COME

This is an age of the world when nations are trembling and convulsed. A mighty influence is abroad, surging and heaving the world, as with an earthquake. And is America safe? Every nation that carries in its bosom great and unredressed injustice has in it the elements of this last convulsion.

For what is this mighty influence thus rousing in all nations and languages those groanings that cannot be uttered, for man's freedom and equality?

O, Church of Christ, read the signs of the times! Is not this power the spirit of Him whose kingdom is yet to come, and whose will to be done on earth as it is in heaven?

But who may abide the day of his appearing? "for that day shall burn as an oven: and he shall appear as a swift witness against those that oppress the hireling in his wages, the widow and the fatherless, and that *turn aside the stranger in his right:* and he shall break in pieces the oppressor."

Are not these dread words for a nation bearing in her bosom so mighty an injustice? Christians! every time that you pray that the kingdom of Christ may come, can you forget that prophecy associates, in dread fellowship, the *day of vengeance* with the year of his redeemed?

A day of grace is yet held out to us. Both North and South have been guilty before God; and the *Christian church* has a heavy account to answer. Not by combining together, to protect injustice and cruelty, and making a common capital of sin, is this Union to be saved,—but by repentance, justice and mercy; for, not surer is the eternal law by which the millstone sinks in the ocean, than that stronger law, by which injustice and cruelty shall bring on nations the wrath of Almighty God!

CHAPTER 4

A WAR FOR ABOLITION OR UNION?

AMERICAN
SOCIAL
MOVEMENTS

Abolition Must Be the Main Goal of the Civil War

FREDERICK DOUGLASS

Frederick Douglass, a former slave, became the leading African American spokesman for abolition during the 1850s. When Douglass joined the abolitionist vanguard, he worked closely with William Lloyd Garrison, the editor of the *Liberator*, the most prominent and effective abolitionist newspaper. Later, Douglass established and edited his own abolitionist newspapers, the *North Star* and *Douglass' Monthly*, to spread his abolitionist message. In this 1861 selection from *Douglass' Monthly*, Douglass argues that abolition must be the main goal of the Civil War because the policy of restoring the Union with slavery in place hangs like a millstone around the necks of all African Americans.

The present policy of our Government is evidently to put down the slaveholding rebellion, and at the same time protect and preserve slavery. This policy hangs like a millstone about the neck of our people. It carries disorder to the very sources of our national activities. Weakness, faint heartedness and inefficiency is the natural result. The mental and moral machinery of mankind cannot long withstand such disorder without serious damage. This policy offends reason, wounds the sensibilities, and shocks the moral sentiments of men. It forces upon us inconsequent conclusions and painful contradictions, while the plain path of duty is obscured and thronged with multiplying difficulties. Let us look this slavery-preserving policy squarely in the face, and search it thoroughly.

Frederick Douglass, "Cast Off the Millstone," *Douglass' Monthly*, 1861.

A War for Abolition

Can the friends of that policy tell us why this should not be an abolition war? Is not abolition plainly forced upon the nation as a necessity of national existence? Are not the rebels determined to make the war on their part a war for the utter destruction of liberty and the complete mastery of slavery over every other right and interest in the land?—And is not an abolition war on our part the natural and logical answer to be made to the rebels? We all know it is. But it is said that for the Government to adopt the abolition policy, would involve the loss of the support of the Union men of the Border Slave States. Grant it, and what is such friendship worth? We are stronger without than with such friendship. It arms the enemy, while it disarms its friends. The fact is indisputable, that so long as slavery is respected and protected by our Government, the slaveholders can carry on the rebellion, and no longer.—Slavery is the stomach of the rebellion. The bread that feeds the rebel army, the cotton that clothes them, and the money that arms them and keeps them supplied with powder and bullets, come from the slaves, who, if consulted as to the use which should be made of their hard earnings, would say, give it to the bottom of the sea rather than do with it this mischief. Strike here, cut off the connection between the fighting master and the working slave, and you at once put an end to this rebellion, because you destroy that which feeds, clothes and arms it. Shall this not be done, because we shall offend the Union men in the border states?

But we have good reasons for believing that it would not offend them. The great mass of Union men in all those Border States are intelligently so. They are men who set a higher value upon the Union than upon slavery. In many instances, they recognize slavery as the thing of all others the most degrading to labor and oppressive towards them. They dare not say so now; but let the government say the word, and even they would unite in sending the vile thing to its grave, and rejoice at the opportunity. Such of them as love slavery better than their country are not now, and have never been, friends of the Union. They belong to the destestable class who do the work of enemies in the garb of friendship, and it would be a real gain to get rid of them. Then look at slavery itself—what good thing has it done that it should be allowed to survive a rebellion of its own creation? Why should the nation pour out its blood and lavish its treasure by the million, consent to protect and preserve the guilty cause of all its troubles? The answer returned to these questions is, that the Constitution does not allow of the exercise of such power. As if this were a time to talk of constitutional power! When a man is well, it would be mayhem to cut off his arm. It would be unconstitutional to do so. But if the arm were shattered and mortifying, it would be quite unconstitutional and criminal not to cut it off. The case is precisely so with Governments. The grand object, end and aim of Government is the preservation of society, and from nothing worse than anarchy. When Governments, through the ordinary channels of civil law, are unable to secure this end, they are thrown back upon military law, and for the time may set aside the civil law precisely to the extent which it may be necessary to do so in order to accomplish the grand object for which Governments are instituted among men. The power, therefore, to abolish slavery is within the objects sought by the Constitution. But if every letter and syllable of the Constitution were a prohibition of abolition, yet if the life of the nation required it, we should be bound by the Constitution to abolish it, because there can be no interest superior to existence and preservation.

AN EVIL POLICY

A very palpable evil involved in the policy of leaving slavery untouched, is that it holds out the idea that we are, in the end, to be treated to another compromise, and the old virus left to heal over, only to fester deeper, and break out more violently again some time not far distant, perhaps, to the utter destruction of the Government for which the people are now spilling their blood and spending their money. If we are to have a compromise and a settlement, why protract the war and prolong the bloodshed? Is it said that no compromise is contemplated? It may be so; but while slavery is admitted to have any right to be

Former slaves join the Union army, hoping that a victory for the North will lead to the abolition of slavery.

protected by our army, it will be impossible not to recognize its right to be protected by Congress; and already we see a binding Republican journal in this State urging the acceptance of the Crittenden Compromise, by which the system of slavery shall be established in all territory south of 36° 30 min. of north latitude. The way to put an end to any farther sham compromises is to put an end to the hateful thing itself, which is the subject of them; and whatever the slave-driving rebels may say, the plain people of the country will accept the proposition of emancipation with the utmost satisfaction.

Another evil of the policy of protecting and preserving slavery, is that it deprives us of the important aid which might be rendered to the Govenment by the four million slaves. These people are repelled by our slaveholding policy. They have their hopes of deliverance from bondage destroyed. They hesitate now; but if our policy is pursued, they will not need to be compelled by Jefferson Davis to fight against us. They will do it from choice, and with a will—deeming it better

"To endure those ills they have,
Than fly to others they know not of."

If they must remain slaves, they would rather fight for than against the masters which we of the North mean to compel them to serve. Who can blame them? They are men, and like men governed by their interests. They are capable of love and hate. They can be friends, and they can be foes. The policy of our Government serves to make them our foes, when it should endeavor by all means to make them our friends and allies.

A third evil of this policy, is the chilling effect it exerts upon the moral sentiment of mankind. Vast is the power of the sympathy of the civilized world. Daniel Webster once said that it was more powerful than "lightning, whirlwind or earthquake."—This vast and invisible power is now evidently not with us. On the briny wing of every eastern gale there comes a depressing chill to the North, while to the South it brings encouragement and hope. Our policy gives the rebels the advantage of seeming to be merely fighting for the right to govern themselves. We divest the war on our part of all those grand elements of progress and philanthropy that naturally win the hearts and command the reverence of all men, and allow it to assume the form of a meaningless display of brute force. The idea that people have a right to govern themselves, whether true or false, has a very strong hold upon the minds of men throughout the world. They naturally side with those who assert this right by force in any part of the world. The example of America has done much to impress this idea upon mankind, and the growing sympathy of the world seems now far more likely to bring some Lafayette with an army of twenty thousand men to aid the rebels, then some Garibaldi to aid the Government in suppressing the rebels. Our slaveholding, slave-catching and slave insurrection policy gives to the South the sympathy which would naturally and certainly flow towards us, and which would be mightier than lightning, whirlwind or earthquake in extinguishing the flames of this momentous slaveholding war.

Another evil arising from this mischievous slaveholding policy, is that it invites the interference of other Governments with our blockade. Break up the blockade, and the war is ended, and the rebels are victorious, and the South is independent. It is already evident that France and England will not long endure a war whose only effect is to starve thousands of their people, slaughter thousands of our own, and sink millions of money. If they are to suffer with us, they will demand—and they have a perfect right to demand—that something shall be gained to the cause of humanity and civilization. Let the war be made an abolition war, and no statesman in England or France would dare even, if inclined, to propose any disturbance of the blockade. Make this an abolition war, and you at once unite the world against the rebels, and in favor of the Government.

The Goal of the War: Abolish Slavery or Preserve the Union?

HORACE GREELEY AND ABRAHAM LINCOLN

In August 1862, Horace Greeley, the editor of the *New York Tribune*, published an editorial in his newspaper urging President Abraham Lincoln to issue an emancipation decree. Greeley's statement, titled "The Prayer of Twenty Millions," was composed as a letter to President Lincoln criticizing his policy of waging a war to reunite the Union without abolishing slavery. A few days later, Lincoln responded to Greeley with a letter in which he articulated his main war goal: first and foremost to preserve the Union. But Lincoln conceded that he would be willing to free some or all American slaves if emancipation would advance his main goal of saving the Union. The president also suggested that although his official duty as president was to save the Union, he personally wished that all men could be free.

*T*o *Abraham Lincoln, President of the United States:*
DEAR SIR: I do not intrude to tell you—for you must know already—that a great proportion of those who triumphed in your election, and of all who desire the unqualified suppression of the rebellion now desolating our country, are sorely disappointed and deeply pained by the policy you seem to be pursuing with regard to the slaves of rebels. I write only to set succinctly and unmistakably before you what we require, what we think we have a right to expect, and of what we complain.
I. We require of you, as the first servant of the Republic, charged especially and preeminently with this duty, that you EXECUTE THE LAWS. . . .

Henry Steele Commager and Milton Cantor, eds., *Documents of American History, Volume 1: To 1898*. Englewood Cliffs, NJ: Prentice-Hall, 1988.

II. We think you are strangely and disastrously remiss in the discharge of your official and imperative duty with regard to the emancipating provisions of the new Confiscation Act. Those provisions were designed to fight Slavery with Liberty. They prescribe that men loyal to the Union, and willing to shed their blood in her behalf, shall no longer be held, with the nation's consent, in bondage to persistent, malignant traitors, who for twenty years have been plotting and for sixteen months have been fighting to divide and destroy our country. Why these traitors should be treated with tenderness by you, to the prejudice of the dearest rights of loyal men, we cannot conceive.

III. We think you are unduly influenced by the councils, the representations, the menaces, of certain fossil politicians hailing from the Border Slave States. Knowing well that the heartily, unconditionally loyal portion of the white citizens of those States do not expect nor desire that Slavery shall be upheld to the prejudice of the Union—(for the truth of which we appeal not only to every Republican residing in those States, but to such eminent loyalists as H. Winter Davis, Parson Brownlow, the Union Central Committee of Baltimore, and to *The Nashville Union*)—we ask you to consider that Slavery is everywhere the inciting cause and sustaining base of treason: the most slaveholding sections of Maryland and Delaware being this day, though under the Union flag, in full sympathy with the rebellion, while the free labor portions of Tennessee and of Texas, though writhing under the bloody heel of treason, are unconquerably loyal to the Union. . . . It seems to us the most obvious truth, that whatever strengthens or fortifies Slavery in the Border States strengthens also treason, and drives home the wedge intended to divide the Union. Had you, from the first, refused to recognize in those States, as here, any other than unconditional loyalty—that which stands for the Union, whatever may become of Slavery—those States would have been, and would be, far more helpful and less troublesome to the defenders of the Union than they have been, or now are.

IV. We think timid counsels in such a crisis calculated to prove perilous, and probably disastrous. It is the duty of a Government so wantonly, wickedly assailed by rebellion as ours has been, to oppose force to force in a defiant, dauntless spirit. It cannot afford to temporize with traitors, nor with semi-traitors. It must not bribe them to behave themselves, nor make them fair promises in the hope of disarming their causeless hostility. Representing a brave and high-spirited people, it can afford to forfeit any thing else better than its own self-respect, or their admiring confidence. For our Government even to seek, after war has been made on it, to dispel the affected apprehensions of armed traitors that their cherished privileges may be assailed by it, is to invite insult and encourage hopes of its own downfall. The rush to arms of Ohio, Indiana, Illinois, is the true answer at once to the rebel raids of John Morgan and the traitorous sophistries of Beriah Magoffin.

V. We complain that the Union cause has suffered, and is now suffering immensely, from mistaken deference to rebel Slavery. Had you, sir, in your Inaugural Address, unmistakably given notice that, in case the rebellion already commenced, were persisted in, and your efforts to preserve the Union and enforce the laws should be resisted by armed force, *you would recognize no loyal person as rightfully held in Slavery by a traitor*, we believe the rebellion would therein have received a staggering if not fatal blow. At that moment, according to the returns of the most recent elections, the Unionists were a large majority of the voters of the slave States. But they were composed in good part of the aged, the feeble, the wealthy, the timid—the young, the reckless, the aspiring, the adventurous, had already been largely lured by the gamblers and negro-traders, the politicians by trade and the conspirators by instinct, into the toils of treason. Had you then proclaimed that rebellion would strike the shackles from the slaves of every traitor, the wealthy and the cautious would have been supplied with a powerful inducement to remain loyal. . . .

VI. We complain that the Confiscation Act which you approved is habitually disregarded by your Generals, and that no word of rebuke for them from you has yet reached the public ear. [General John] Frémont's Proclamation and Hunter's Order favoring Emancipation were promptly annulled by you; while Halleck's Number Three, forbidding fugitives from slavery to

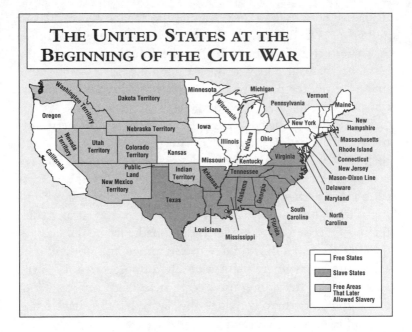

THE UNITED STATES AT THE BEGINNING OF THE CIVIL WAR

rebels to come within his lines—an order as unmilitary as inhuman, and which received the hearty approbation of every traitor in America—with scores of like tendency, have never provoked even your remonstrance. . . . And finally, we complain that you, Mr. President, elected as a Republican, knowing well what an abomination Slavery is, and how emphatically it is the core and essence of this atrocious rebellion, seem never to interfere with these atrocities, and never give a direction to your military subordinates, which does not appear to have been conceived in the interest of Slavery rather than of Freedom. . . .

VIII. On the face of this wide earth, Mr. President, there is not one disinterested, determined, intelligent champion of the Union cause who does not feel that all attempts to put down the rebellion and at the same time uphold its inciting cause are preposterous and futile—that the rebellion, if crushed out tomorrow, would be renewed within a year if Slavery were left in full vigor—that army officers who remain to this day devoted to Slavery can at best be but half-way loyal to the Union—and that every hour of deference to Slavery is an hour of added and deepened peril to the Union. I appeal to the testimony of your ambassadors in Europe. It is freely at your service, not at mine. Ask them to tell you candidly whether the seeming subserviency of your policy to the slaveholding, slavery-upholding interest, is not the perplexity, the despair of statesmen of all parties, and be admonished by the general answer!

IX. I close as I began with the statement that what an immense majority of the loyal millions of your countrymen require of you is a frank, declared, unqualified, ungrudging execution of the laws of the land, more especially of the Confiscation Act. That act gives freedom to the slaves of rebels coming within our lines, or whom those lines may at any time inclose—we ask you to render it due obedience by publicly requiring all your subordinates to recognize and obey it. The rebels are everywhere using the late anti-negro riots in the North, as they have long used your officers' treatment of negroes in the South, to convince the slaves that they have nothing to hope from a Union success—that we mean in that case to sell them into a bitter bondage to defray the cost of the war. Let them impress this as a truth on the great mass of their ignorant and credulous bondmen, and the Union will never be restored—never. We cannot conquer ten millions of people united in solid phalanx against us, powerfully aided by Northern sympathizers and European allies. We must have scouts, guides, spies, cooks, teamsters, diggers, and choppers from the blacks of the South, whether we allow them to fight for us or not, or we shall be baffled and repelled. As one of the millions who would gladly have avoided this struggle at any sacrifice but that of principle and honor, but who now feel that the triumph of the Union is indispensable not only to the existence of our country but to the well-being of mankind, I entreat you to render a hearty and unequivocal obedience to the law of the land.

Yours, HORACE GREELEY.

LINCOLN'S RESPONSE

Hon. Horace Greeley:

DEAR SIR: I have just read yours of the nineteenth, addressed to myself through the New-York *Tribune*. If there be in it any statements or assumptions of fact which I may know to be erroneous, I do not now and here controvert them. If there be in it any inferences which I may believe to be falsely drawn, I do not now and here argue against them. If there be perceptible in it an impatient and dictatorial tone, I waive it in deference to an old friend, whose heart I have always supposed to be right.

As to the policy I "seem to be pursuing," as you say, I have not meant to leave any one in doubt.

I would save the Union. I would save it the shortest way under the Constitution. The sooner the National authority can be restored, the nearer the Union will be "the Union as it was." If there be those who would not save the Union unless they could at the same time *save* Slavery, I do not agree with them. If there be those who would not save the Union unless they could at the same time *destroy* Slavery, I do not agree with them. My paramount object in this struggle *is* to save the Union, and is *not* either to save or destroy Slavery. If I could save the Union without freeing *any* slave, I would do it; and if I could save it by freeing *all* the slaves, I would do it; and if I could do it by freeing some and leaving others alone, I would also do that. What I do about Slavery and the colored race, I do because I believe it helps to save this Union; and what I forbear, I forbear because I do *not* believe it would help to save the Union. I shall do *less* whenever I shall believe what I am doing hurts the cause, and I shall do *more* whenever I shall believe doing more will help the cause. I shall try to correct errors when shown to be errors; and I shall adopt new views so fast as they shall appear to be true views. I have here stated my purpose according to my view of *official* duty, and I intend no modification of my oft-expressed *personal* wish that all men, everywhere, could be free.

Yours,

A. LINCOLN.

Lincoln Moves Toward Emancipation

JOHN HOPE FRANKLIN

John Hope Franklin, a prominent scholar of African American history, has authored several signal books on the Civil War era, including *From Slavery to Freedom: A History of the American Negro* and *The Emancipation Proclamation*. In this excerpt from *The Emancipation Proclamation*, Franklin traces Abraham Lincoln's movement toward emancipation during the Civil War. According to Franklin, Lincoln moved cautiously toward abolition—first discussing the issue with his advisers and the members of his cabinet, then deciding, during the summer of 1862, to compose an emancipation decree, which he shared with his advisers before announcing it to the American public. According to Franklin, Lincoln might have been influenced by abolition activists, but the final decision to free the slaves was Lincoln's.

The road that led to the issuing of the Preliminary Emancipation Proclamation was a long and difficult one. It was marked by an incredible amount of pressure on Abraham Lincoln, pressure that began the day Sumter fell and that did not relent until his decision was announced on September 22, 1862. It is not possible to weigh the effects of the pressures created by hardheaded generals who would set slaves free in order to break the back of the Confederacy. One cannot know what impressions the procession of the Charles Sumners, the Orestes Brownsons and the religious deputations made on the President as they came by day and by night to tell him what he should do about slavery. Did a [Horace] Greeley editorial or a [Frederick]

John Hope Franklin, *The Emancipation Proclamation*. Garden City, NY: Doubleday & Company, Inc., 1963.

Douglass speech sway him? One cannot know the answers to these questions, for Lincoln, the only one who could do so, never gave the answers. He was doubtlessly impressed by all arguments that were advanced, and he took all of them "under advisement." But the final decision was his.

LINCOLN BELIEVED SLAVERY WAS WRONG

Lincoln needed no convincing that slavery was wrong, and he had been determined for many years to strike a blow for freedom if the opportunity ever came his way. As a young man he told a New Orleans group in 1831, "If I ever get a chance to hit that thing, I'll hit it hard." He fully appreciated, moreover, the disastrous effect of slavery on national development and on the national character. He told a Cincinnati audience in 1842 that "Slavery and oppression must cease, or American liberty must perish."

Lincoln was irritated by any suggestion that he was "soft" on the question of slavery. "I am naturally anti-slavery," he wrote a friend shortly after the beginning of his second term. "If slavery is not wrong, nothing is wrong.... And yet I have never understood that the Presidency conferred upon me an unrestricted right to act officially on this judgment and feeling.... And I aver that to this day [April 4, 1864] I have done no official act in mere deference to my abstract judgment and feeling on slavery."

THE LEGALITY OF EMANCIPATION

Thus Lincoln was troubled by unanswered questions regarding the legality as well as the effect of emancipation on the course of the war and on the peace and well-being of the country. Who could know if the soldiers of Kentucky would lay down their arms if Lincoln set the slaves free? Greeley replied, "Let them do it. The cause of Union will be stronger, if Kentucky should secede with the rest, than it is now." It was not quite so simple, when one had the responsibility for shaping the course of the war and preserving the life of the Union. What would happen to the Negroes once they are free? Who would take care of them? These were questions that Lincoln asked over and over. Frederick Douglass, the runaway slave who had been a resounding success on two continents, had the answer. "Let them take care of themselves, as others do." If the black man could take care of his master and mistress, he could take care of himself. Should the freed Negroes be allowed to remain in the United States? "Yes," Douglass replied, "they wouldn't take up more room than they do now." Facile, even witty answers were not enough for the troubled Lincoln.

Since Lincoln was quite certain that sooner or later, in war or in peace, the slaves would be free, he gave much attention to what should be done with them. "You and we are different races," he told a group of Negroes in August 1862. "Whether it is right or wrong I need not discuss, but this physical difference is a great disadvantage to us both, as I think your race suffer very greatly, many of them by living among us, while ours suffer from your presence. In a word we suffer on each side. If this be admitted, it affords a reason at least why we should be separated." Freedom called for colonization, Lincoln felt; and it seemed to occupy his attention about as much as any single matter during the first two years of the war.

Colonizing the Freed Slaves

As Lincoln moved toward a policy of emancipation, his interest in colonizing Negroes in some other parts of the world quickened. Indeed, it is almost possible to measure his approach to emancipation by studying the increasing intensity of his efforts to formulate a feasible program of colonization. In 1854 he said that his first impulse "would be to free all the slaves and send them back to Liberia, to their own native land." In his first annual message he proposed colonization for Negroes freed in the course of the war. He urged colonization for the slaves of the District of Columbia when they were freed in April 1862. He spearheaded the legislation in July 1862 that appropriated a half million dollars to colonize slaves of disloyal masters.

When Lincoln met the group of Negroes in August 1862, and talked to them about colonization, he had already decided to issue the Proclamation. This very decision seemed to make him all the more anxious about colonization. He asked them to give serious consideration to the idea of colonizing in Central America. The Negroes showed little enthusiasm for the proposal. In the following two weeks he discussed colonization in Chiriqui, a province in Panama, with several individuals and with members of the Cabinet. At the end of the month he decided to abandon the project because of lack of support. He was not altogether discouraged, and for the next several months he continued his vain attempts to gain support for colonization.

LINCOLN PLANS FOR EMANCIPATION

Early in 1862 Lincoln reached the decision that either he or Congress should emancipate the slaves. By March he had composed the draft of a special message to Congress recommending compensated emancipation. He read it to Senator Sumner, who was not enthusiastic about it because it called for gradual emancipation. Neither Congress nor the Delaware leaders upon whom he urged compensated emancipation were any more enthusiastic than Sumner. While Congress passed a resolution embodying the President's recommendations, it made no serious attempt to implement them.

Lincoln later admitted his awareness of pressures, but he never admitted the effect of them on his decision. He said that he forbade [General John] Frémont's and [General David] Hunter's attempts at military emancipation because he did not then think it an indispensable necessity. When the border states declined his appeal to accept compensated emancipation, he was driven to the "alternative of either surrendering the Union, and with it, the Constitution, or of laying a strong hand upon the colored element." He chose the latter. In doing so he hoped for greater gain than loss, but of this he was not entirely confident.

The best evidence supports the view that it was in the late spring of 1862 that the President decided to issue a proclamation freeing the slaves. "Things had gone on from bad to worse," he said, "until I felt that we had reached the end of our rope on the plan of operations we had been pursuing; that we had about played our last card, and must change our tactics, or lose the game!" It was then that he "determined on the adoption of the emancipation policy; and without consultation with, or knowledge of the Cabinet, I prepared the original draft of the proclamation. . . ."

DRAFTING AN EMANCIPATION ANNOUNCEMENT

Lincoln was a frequent visitor to the telegraph room of the War Department. He went there almost daily to receive the reports of the progress of the war and to get away from the turmoil and distraction of the White House, where he had no privacy. Thomas T. Eckert, who was in charge of the telegraph office, was understanding and unobtrusive. Lincoln usually sat at Eckert's desk while at the telegraph office. Early one June morning, Lincoln dropped into the office and asked Eckert for some paper on which to write something special. He sat down and began to write. "He would look out of the window a while," Eckert later reported, "and then put his pen to paper, but he did not write much at once. He would study between times and when he had made up his mind he would put down a line or two, and then sit quiet for a few minutes. After a time he would resume his writing. . . ."

On that first day Lincoln did not fill one sheet of the paper Eckert had given him. When he left he asked Eckert to keep what he had written and not to show it to anyone. On the following day when he returned, he asked for the paper, which Eckert kept in a locked desk; and he began to write. "This he did every day for several weeks." On some days he did not write more than a line or two, and Eckert observed that he had put question marks in the margin. Each day he would read over what he had written and revise it, "studying carefully each sentence." Eckert later said that he did not know what the President was writing until he had finished the draft. Then, for the first time, he told Eckert that he had been writing an order "giving freedom to the slaves in the South for the purpose of hastening the end of the war." He then explained that he had been able to work more quietly and could better command his thoughts at the telegraph office than at the White House, where he was frequently interrupted.

LINCOLN CONSULTS HIS ADVISERS

Within the next few weeks Lincoln widened the circle of confidants with whom he discussed the Proclamation. He had many talks with [Edwin] Stanton, his Secretary of War, about the possible use of Negroes as soldiers. Stanton had the distinct impression that Lincoln was planning to emancipate the slaves at an early date. On May 28 he predicted to Senator [Charles] Sumner that a decree of emancipation would be issued within two months. Although Lincoln was as yet unwilling to arm the slaves, he began to discuss with his advisers the matter of their

President Lincoln (center) visits a Union camp in Sharpsburg, Maryland, in October 1862, shortly before he issued the Emancipation Proclamation.

emancipation *and* their arming. Stanton, an ardent protagonist of both propositions, seemed to be more optimistic as spring gave way to summer in 1862.

On June 18, 1862, the President had a busy day. He received many visitors and, as usual, he fretted over reports of the activity or inactivity of Union troops. To General Henry W. Halleck at Corinth, Mississippi, he sent a message inquiring about the progress of the proposed expedition toward East Tennessee. To [General George] McClellan he sent a curt message saying that he could better dispose of things if he knew about what day McClellan could attack Richmond. Things, indeed, seemed to be going from bad to worse. To get away from it all the President had his horse saddled and, with Vice-President Hannibal Hamlin, rode out to the Soldiers' Home for his evening meal. After dinner the two men retired to the library and talked behind locked doors. According to Hamlin the President began the conversation by saying, "Mr. Hamlin, you have been repeatedly urging me to issue a proclamation of emancipation freeing the slaves. I have concluded to yield to your advice in the matter and that of other friends,—at the same time, as I may say, following my own judgment. Now listen to me as I read this paper. We will correct it together as I go on."

The President then opened a drawer in his desk and took out the draft of the Proclamation. He read it slowly, during which time the Vice-President made no interruptions. When he had finished, Hamlin said that he had no criticism. Lincoln could hardly believe that Hamlin regarded the document as perfect. "At least you can make some suggestions," Lincoln urged. Finally, Hamlin reported, he did make "three suggestions, two of which Mr. Lincoln accepted." He declined to make known what his suggestions were, insisting that the Emancipation Proclamation was the President's "own act, and no one else can claim any credit whatever in connection with it."

INFORMING THE CABINET

The death of young James Hutchison Stanton, Stanton's infant son, occurred at about the same time in July, 1862, as McClellan's retreat from Richmond. Lincoln was grieved by both events, and his depressed state was apparent to his associates. He invited the Secretary of the Navy, Gideon Welles, and the Secretary of State, William H. Seward, to accompany him in the Presidential carriage to the infant's funeral. It was during this ride, on July 13, that Lincoln first mentioned his proposed emancipation proclamation to these highly placed advisers. The President "dwelt earnestly on the gravity, importance, and delicacy of the movement, said he had given it much thought and had about come to the conclusion that it was a military necessity absolutely essential for the salvation of the Union, that we must free the slaves or be ourselves subdued. . . ."

Welles recorded in his diary that Lincoln told them that this was the first time that he had mentioned the subject to anyone. The President invited the two men to state frankly how the proposition struck them. Seward, never lacking a response, said that the subject involved consequences so vast and momentous that he wished more time for mature reflection before giving a decisive answer. His offhand opinion, however, was that the measure was "perfectly justifiable" and perhaps might be expedient and necessary. Welles concurred in this view.

During the ride of some two or three miles beyond Georgetown the three men returned to the subject several times. When they returned to the city the President asked Seward and Welles, as they took their leave, to give the matter their "specific and deliberate attention." As for himself he was firm in his conviction that something must be done.

It was hardly accurate to say that Lincoln had never discussed the matter with anyone. One wonders if Welles' memory was playing tricks on him or if the President's agitated state caused him to speak inaccurately. It was, however, accurate for Welles to declare that it was a new departure for the President to state categorically that he intended to emancipate the slaves. Heretofore, as Welles stated, whenever the matter arose, the President had been "prompt and emphatic in denouncing any interference by the General Government with the subject." The reverses before Richmond and the formidable power and dimensions of the rebellion were forcing the Administration to adopt extraordinary measures to preserve the Union. The proposed emancipation of the slaves fell into the category of extraordinary measures.

The formal solicitation of advice from the Cabinet came at the meeting on July 22, a scarce ten days after the momentous discussion during the funeral ride. When the meeting was called to order, all members were present except Montgomery Blair, the Postmaster General, who arrived during the meeting. The President informed the Cabinet that he had resolved to issue a proclamation emancipating the slaves. His decision in the matter was firm, he assured them. He therefore had called them together to inform them and to solicit their suggestions regarding language and timing.

AN EMANCIPATION DECREE

The President then proceeded to read the following document:

> In pursuance of the sixth section of the act of Congress entitled "An act to suppress insurrection and to punish treason and rebellion, to seize and confiscate property of rebels, and for other purposes" Approved July 17, 1862, and which act, and the Joint Resolution explanatory thereof, are herewith published, I, Abraham Lincoln, President of the United States, do hereby proclaim to, and warn all persons within the contemplation of said sixth section to cease participating in, aiding, countenancing, or abetting the existing rebellion, or any rebellion against the government of the United States, and to return to their proper allegiance to the United States, on pain of the forfeitures and seizures, as within and by [the] sixth section provided.

> And I hereby make known that it is my purpose, upon the next meeting of congress, to again recommend the adoption of a practical measure for tendering aid to the free choice or rejection, of any and all States which may then be recognizing and sustaining the authority of the United States, and which may then have voluntarily adopted, or thereafter may voluntarily adopt, gradual abolishment of slavery within such

State or States—that the object is to practically restore, thenceforward to be maintain[ed], the constitutional relation between the general government, and each, and all the states, wherein that relation is now suspended, or disturbed; and that, for this object, the war, as it has been, will be, prossecuted. And, as a fit and necessary military measure for effecting this object, I, as Commander-in-Chief of the Army and Navy of the United States, do order and declare that on the first day of January in the year of Our Lord one thousand eight hundred and sixtythree, all persons held as slaves within any state or states, wherein the constitutional authority of the United States shall not then be practically recognized, submitted to, and maintained, shall then, thenceforward, and forever, be free.

The Emancipation Proclamation

ABRAHAM LINCOLN

Abraham Lincoln, a native of Kentucky who migrated to Illinois, was the son of poor and hardly literate farmers. Determined to become something other than a farmer, Lincoln, as a young man, studied law and later entered politics. After serving in the Illinois legislature, Lincoln served a single term in the House of Representatives, then retired from politics to work as an attorney. The great slavery debates of the 1850s, particularly the dispute over the Kansas-Nebraska Act, beckoned Lincoln back into politics. Antislavery but not an abolitionist, Lincoln argued that slavery should remain legal in the South where it already existed, but it should not be introduced into new states or territories. After an unsuccessful campaign to win an Illinois Senate seat in 1858, Lincoln, in 1860, ran for president and won. As a result of the election of Lincoln, several southern states voted to secede from the Union. A month after Lincoln took office, the Civil War began. From the beginning, abolitionists urged Lincoln to make slavery a casualty of the war, but Lincoln maintained that his main goal in the war was to restore the Union, not to abolish slavery. Eighteen months into the war, however, Lincoln, decided to free the slaves in the states in rebellion. After warning the South of his intentions, Lincoln, on January 1, 1863, issued the Emancipation Proclamation, an act of military necessity that freed the slaves in the states in rebellion and invited African American freedmen to join the Union army.

Whereas, on the twentysecond day of September, in the year of our Lord one thousand eight hundred and sixty two, a proclamation was issued by the President of the United States, containing, among other things, the following, towit:

Abraham Lincoln, "Emancipation Proclamation," January 1, 1863.

"That on the first day of January, in the year of our Lord one thousand eight hundred and sixty-three, all persons held as slaves within any State or designated part of a State, the people whereof shall then be in rebellion against the United States, shall be then, thenceforward and forever free; and the Executive Government of the United States, including the military and naval authority thereof, will recognize and maintain the freedom of such persons, and will do no act or acts to repress such persons, or any of them, in any efforts they may make for their actual freedom.

"That the Executive will, on the first day of January aforesaid, by proclamation, designate the States and parts of States, if any, in which people thereof, respectively, shall then be in rebellion against the United States; and the fact that any State, or the people thereof, shall on that day be, in good faith, represented in the Congress of the United States by members chosen thereto at elections wherein a majority of the qualified voters of such State shall have participated, shall, in the absence of strong countervailing testimony, be deemed conclusive evidence that such State, and the people thereof, are not then in rebellion against the United States."

Now, therefore I, Abraham Lincoln, President of the United States, by virtue of the power in me vested as Commander-in-Chief, of the Army and Navy of the United States in time of actual armed rebellion against authority and government of the United States, and as a fit and necessary war measure for suppressing said rebellion, do, on this first day of January, in the year of our Lord one thousand eight hundred and sixty three, and in accordance with my purpose so to do publicly proclaimed for the full period of one hundred days, from the day first above mentioned, order and designate as the States and parts of States wherein the people thereof respectively, are this day in rebellion against the United States, the following towit:

Arkansas, Texas, Louisiana (except the Parishes of St. Bernard, Plaquemines, Jefferson, St. Johns, St. Charles, St. James, Ascension, Assumption, Terrebonne, Lafourche, St. Mary, St. Martin, and Orleans, including the City of New-Orleans), Mississippi, Alabama, Florida, Georgia, South-Carolina, North-Carolina, and Virginia, (except the fortyeight counties designated as West Virginia, and also the counties of Berkley, Accomac, Northampton, Elizabeth-City, York, Princess Ann, and Norfolk, including the cities of Norfolk & Portsmouth); and which excepted parts are, for the present, left precisely as if this proclamation were not issued.

And by virtue of the power, and for the purpose aforesaid, I do order and declare that all persons held as slaves within said designated States, and parts of States, are, and hence-forward shall be free; and that the Executive government of the United States, including the military and naval authorities thereof, will

A Day of Jubilee

On January 1, 1863, President Abraham Lincoln issued the Emancipation Proclamation, freeing slaves in the states in rebellion against the Union. The day was widely celebrated in African American communities. On that day, Charlotte Forten, a free-born African American, was doing volunteer work at an army camp for African American soldiers on a Union-held island off the coast of South Carolina. She recorded her feelings on that day in her diary.

Thursday, New Year's Day, 1863. The most glorious day this nation has yet seen I think. I rose early—an event here—and early we started. . . . I *cannot* give a regular chronicle of the day. It is impossible. I was in such a state of excitement. It all seemed, and seems still, like a brilliant dream. . . . The exercises commenced. . . . Then the beautiful flags presented by Dr. Cheever's Church were presented to Col. H[igginson] for the Reg. in an excellent and enthusiastic speech, by Rev. Mr. French. Immediately at the conclusion, some of the colored people—of their own accord sang recognize and maintain the freedom of said persons.

And I hereby enjoin upon the people so declared to be free to abstain from all violence, unless in necessary self-defence; and I recommend to them that, in all cases when allowed, they labor faithfully for reasonable wages.

And I further declare and make known, that such persons of suitable condition, will be received into the armed service of the United States to garrison forts, positions, stations, and other places, and to man vessels of all sorts in said service.

AN ACT OF MILITARY NECESSITY

And upon this act, sincerely believed to be an act of justice, warranted by the Constitution, upon military necessity, I invoke

"My Country Tis of Thee." It was a touching and beautiful incident, and Col. Higginson, in accepting the flags made it the occasion of some happy remarks. He said that *that* tribute was far more effecting than any speech he c'ld make. He spoke for some time, and all said that he was grand, glorious. He seemed inspired. Nothing could have been better, more perfect. . . . The Dress Parade the first I have ever seen—delighted me. It was a brilliant sight—the lone line of men in their brilliant uniforms, with bayonets gleaming in the sunlight. . . . To me it was a grand triumph—that black regiment doing itself honor in the sight of the white officers, many of whom, doubtless "came to scoff." It was typical of what the race, so long downtrodden and degraded will yet achieve on this continent. . . . Ah, what a grand, glorious day this has been. The dawn of freedom which it heralds may not break upon us at once; but it will surely come. . . .

Louis P. Masur, ed., *"The Real War Will Never Get in the Books": Selections from Writers During the Civil War.* New York: Oxford University Press, 1993.

the considerate judgment of mankind, and the gracious favor of Almighty God.

In witness whereof, I have hereunto set my hand and caused the seal of the United States to be affixed.

Done at the City of Washington, this first day of January, in the year of our Lord one thousand eight hundred and sixty three, and of the Independence of the United States of America the eighty-seventh.

Extolling Lincoln's Emancipation Decree

HARRIET BEECHER STOWE

Harriet Beecher Stowe, the author of *Uncle Tom's Cabin*, grew up in a famous abolitionist family. Her father, Lyman Beecher, and her brother, Henry Ward Beecher, were nationally known clergymen who railed against slavery from their pulpits. After publishing *Uncle Tom's Cabin*, Stowe, too, became prominent in the abolitionist movement. She lectured on the evils of slavery and spread the abolitionist message in newspaper articles and private letters. Like other abolitionists, Stowe celebrated the issuance of the Emancipation Proclamation on January 1, 1863. In this article, which appeared in *Atlantic Monthly* in January 1863, Stowe shares her excitement about Abraham Lincoln's emancipation decree with abolitionists in Great Britain. Stowe traces the nation's movement toward abolition, which culminated with the Emancipation Proclamation.

The time has come ... when such an astonishing page has been turned in the anti-slavery history of America, that the women of our country, feeling that the great anti-slavery work to which their English sisters exhorted them is almost done, may properly and naturally feel moved to reply to their appeal, and lay before them the history of what has occurred since the receipt of their affectionate and Christian address.

Your address reached us just as a great moral conflict was coming to its intensest point.

AN INTOLERABLE SITUATION

The agitation kept up by the anti-slavery portion of America, by England, and by the general sentiment of humanity in Eu-

Harriet Beecher Stowe, "A Reply," *Atlantic Monthly*, January 1863.

rope, had made the situation of the slaveholding aristocracy intolerable. As one of them at the time expressed it, they felt themselves under the ban of the civilized world. Two courses only were open to them: to abandon slave institutions, the sources of their wealth and political power, or to assert them with such an overwhelming national force as to compel the respect and assent of mankind. They chose the latter.

To this end they determined to seize on and control all the resources of the Federal Government, and to spread their institutions through new States and Territories until the balance of power should fall into their hands and they should be able to force slavery into all the Free States.

A leading Southern senator boasted that he would yet call the roll of his slaves on Bunker Hill; and, for a while, the political successes of the Slave Power were such as to suggest to New England that this was no impossible event.

They repealed the Missouri Compromise, which had hitherto stood, like the Chinese wall; between our Northwestern Territories and the irruptions of slaveholding barbarians.

Then came the struggle between Freedom and Slavery in the new Territory,—the battle for Kansas, and Nebraska, fought with fire and sword and blood, where a race of men, of whom John Brown was the immortal type, acted over again the courage, the perseverence, and the military religious ardor of the old Covenanters of Scotland, and, like them, redeemed the Ark of Liberty at the price of their own blood and blood dearer than their own.

Lincoln's Election Initiates a Crisis

The time of the Presidential canvass which elected Mr. Lincoln was the crisis of this great battle. The conflict had become narrowed down to the one point of the extension of slave-territory. If the slaveholders could get States enough, they could control and rule; if they were outnumbered by Free States, their institutions, by the very law of their nature, would die of suffocation. Therefore, Fugitive-Slave Law, District of Columbia, Inter-State Slave-Trade, and what not, were all thrown out of sight for a grand rally on this vital point. A President was elected pledged to opposition to this one thing alone,—a man known to be in favor of the Fugitive-Slave Law and other so-called compromises of the Constitution, but honest and faithful in his determination on this one subject. That this was indeed the vital point was shown by the result. The moment Lincoln's election was ascertained, the slaveholders resolved to destroy the Union they could no longer control.

They met and organized a Confederacy which they openly declared to be the first republic founded on the right and determination of the white man to enslave the black man, and, spreading their banners, declared themselves to the Christian world of the nineteenth century as a nation organized with the full purpose and intent of perpetuating slavery.

A WAR OVER SLAVERY OR UNION

But in the course of the struggle that followed, it became important for the new Confederation to secure the assistance of foreign powers, and infinite pains were then taken to blind and bewilder the mind of England as to the real issues of the conflict in America.

It has been often and earnestly asserted that slavery had nothing to do with this conflict; that it was a mere struggle for power; that the only object was to restore the Union as it was, with all its abuses. It is to be admitted that expressions have proceeded from the National Administration which naturally gave rise to misapprehension, and therefore we beg to speak to you on this subject more fully.

And, first, the declaration of the Confederate States themselves is proof enough that, whatever may be declared on the other side, the maintenance of slavery is regarded by them as the vital object of their movement. . . . On the other hand, the declarations of the President and the Republican party, as to their intention to restore "the Union as it was," require an explanation. It is the doctrine of the Republican party, that Freedom is national and Slavery sectional; that the Constitution of the United States was designed for the promotion of liberty, and not of slavery; that its framers contemplated the gradual abolition of slavery; and that in the hands of an anti-slavery majority it could be so wielded as peaceably to extinguish this great evil.

They reasoned thus. Slavery ruins land, and requires fresh territory for profitable working. Slavery increases a dangerous population, and requires an expansion of this population for safety. Slavery, then, being hemmed in by impassable limits, emancipation in each State becomes a necessity.

By restoring the Union as it was the Republican party meant the Union in the sense contemplated by the original framers of it, who, as has been admitted by [Alexander] Stephens, . . . were from principle opposed to slavery. It was, then, restoring a *status* in which, by the inevitable operation of natural laws, peaceful emancipation would become a certainty.

STEPS TAKEN TO ABOLISH SLAVERY

In the mean while, during the past year, the Republican Administration, with all the unwonted care of organizing an army and navy, and conducting military operations on an immense scale, have proceeded to demonstrate the feasibility of overthrowing slavery by purely Constitutional measures. To this end they have instituted a series of movements which have made this year more fruitful in anti-slavery triumphs than any other since the emancipation of the British West Indies.

The District of Columbia, as belonging strictly to the National Government, and to no separate State, has furnished a fruitful subject of remonstrance from British Christians with America. We have abolished slavery there, and thus wiped out the only blot of territorial responsibility on our escutcheon.

By another act, equally grand in principle, and far more important in its results, slavery is forever excluded from the Territories of the United States.

By another act, America has consummated the long-delayed treaty with Great Britain for the suppression of the slave-trade. In ports where slave-vessels formerly sailed with the connivance of the port-officers the Administration has placed men who stand up to their duty, and for the first time in our history the slave-trader is convicted and hung as a pirate. This abominable secret traffic has been wholly demolished by the energy of the Federal Government.

Lastly, and more significant still, the United States Government has in its highest official capacity taken distinct anti-slavery ground, and presented to the country a plan of peaceable emancipation with suitable compensation. This noble-spirited and generous offer has been urged on the Slaveholding States by the Chief Executive with an earnestness and sincerity of which history in aftertimes will make honorable account in recording the events of Mr. Lincoln's administration.

Now, when a President and Administration who have done all these things declare their intention of restoring *"the Union as it was,"* ought not the world fairly to interpret their words by their actions and their avowed principles? Is it not *necessary* to infer that they mean by it the Union as it was in the intent of its anti-slavery framers, under which, by the exercise of normal Constitutional powers, slavery should be peaceably abolished?

We are aware that this theory of the Constitution has been disputed by certain Abolitionists; but it is conceded, as you have seen, by the Secessionists. Whether it be a just theory or not is, however, nothing to our purpose at present. We only assert that such is the professed belief of the present Administration of the United States, and such are the acts by which they have illustrated their belief.

ACTS OF WAR

But this is but half the story of the anti-slavery triumphs of this year. We have shown you what has been done for freedom by the simple use of the ordinary Constitutional forces of the Union. We are now to show you what has been done to the same end by the Constitutional war-power of the nation.

By this power it has been this year decreed that every slave of a Rebel who reaches the lines of our army becomes a free man; that all slaves found deserted by masters become free men; that every slave employed in any service for the United States thereby obtains his liberty; and that every slave employed against the United States in any capacity obtains his liberty; and lest the army should contain officers disposed to remand slaves to their masters, the power of judging and delivering up slaves is denied to army-officers, and all such acts are made penal.

By this act, the Fugitive-Slave Law is for all present purposes practically repealed. With this understanding and provision, wherever our armies march, they carry liberty with them. For be it remembered that our army is almost entirely a volunteer one, and that the most zealous and ardent volunteers are those who have been for years fighting with tongue and pen the Abolition battle. So marked is the character of our soldiers in this respect, that they are now familiarly designated in the official military dispatches of the Confederate States as "The Abolitionists." Conceive the results, when an army, so empowered by national law, marches through a slave-territory. One regiment alone has to our certain knowledge liberated two thousand slaves during the past year, and this regiment is but one out of hundreds. . . .

It is conceded on all sides, that, wherever our armies have had occupancy, there slavery has been practically abolished. The fact was recognized by President Lincoln in his last appeal to the loyal Slave States to consummate emancipation.

Another noticeable act of our Government in behalf of Liberty is the official provision it makes for the wants of the thousands of helpless human beings thus thrown upon our care. Taxed with the burden of an immense war, with the care of thousands of sick and wounded, the United States Government has cheerfully voted rations for helpless slaves, no less than wages to the helpful ones. The United States Government pays teachers to instruct them, and overseers to guide their industrial efforts. A free-labor experiment is already in successful operation among the beautiful sea-islands in the neighborhood of Beaufort, which, even under most disadvantageous circumstances, is fast demonstrating how much more efficiently men will work from hope and liberty than from fear and constraint. Thus, even amid the roar of cannon and the confusion of war, cotton-planting, as a free-labor institution, is beginning its instant life, to grow hereafter to a glorious manhood.

Lastly, the great, decisive measure of the war has approached, —*The President's Proclamation of Emancipation.*

This also has been much misunderstood and misrepresented in England. It has been said to mean virtually this:—Be loyal, and you shall keep your slaves; rebel, and they shall be free.

But let us remember what we have just seen of the purpose and meaning of the Union to which the rebellious States are invited back. It is to a Union which has abolished slavery in the District of Columbia, and interdicted slavery in the Territories,—which vigorously represses the slave-trade, and hangs the convicted slaver as a pirate,—which necessitates emancipation by denying expansion to slavery, and facilitates it by the offer of compensation. Any Slaveholding States which should return to such a Union might fairly be supposed to return with the purpose of peaceable emancipation. The President's Proclamation simply means this:—Come in, and emancipate peaceably with compensation; stay out, and I emancipate, nor will I protect you from the consequences.

CHAPTER 5

FROM EMANCIPATION TO CIVIL RIGHTS

AMERICAN
SOCIAL
MOVEMENTS

Voting Rights for the Freedmen

FREDERICK DOUGLASS

Frederick Douglass, a former slave who became an abolitionist author, editor, and orator, was the most famous African American of the nineteenth century. While agitating for the immediate emancipation of all American slaves, Douglass also argued persistently for equal rights for all African American freedmen. When it became clear that American slavery would become a casualty of the Civil War, Douglass sounded the call for voting rights for the free and newly freed slaves. Douglass established and edited two newspapers, the *North Star* and *Douglass' Monthly*, to articulate his political message. The statement below is the text of a speech that Douglass delivered to the annual meeting of the Massachusetts Anti-Slavery Society in 1865. In this oration, Douglass outlines the case for suffrage for African Americans in the aftermath of the Civil War.

I have had but one idea for the last three years to present to the American people, and the phraseology in which I clothe it is the old abolition phraseology. I am for the "immediate, unconditional, and universal" enfranchisement of the black man, in every State in the Union. Without this, his liberty is a mockery; without this, you might as well almost retain the old name of slavery for his condition; for in fact, if he is not the slave of the individual master, he is the slave of society, and holds his liberty as a privilege, not as a right. He is at the mercy of the mob, and has no means of protecting himself.

It may be objected, however, that this pressing of the Negro's right to suffrage is premature. Let us have slavery abolished, it may be said, let us have labor organized, and then, in the natural

Frederick Douglass, speech before the annual meeting of the Massachusetts Anti-Slavery Society, 1865.

course of events, the right of suffrage will be extended to the Negro. I do not agree with this. The constitution of the human mind is such, that if it once disregards the conviction forced upon it by a revelation of truth, it requires the exercise of a higher power to produce the same conviction afterwards. The American people are now in tears. The Shenandoah has run blood—the best blood of the North. All around Richmond, the blood of New England and of the North has been shed—of your sons, your brothers and your fathers. We all feel, in the existence of this Rebellion, that judgments terrible, wide-spread, far-reaching, overwhelming, are abroad in the land; and we feel, in view of these judgments, just now, a disposition to learn righteousness. This is the hour. Our streets are in mourning, tears are falling at every fireside, and under the chastisement of this Rebellion we have almost come up to the point of conceding this great, this all important right of suffrage. I fear that if we fail to do it now, if abolitionists fail to press it now, we may not see, for centuries to come, the same disposition that exists at this moment. Hence, I say, now is the time to press this right.

WHY THE FREED SLAVES MUST VOTE

It may be asked, "Why do you want it? Some men have got along very well without it. Women have not this right." Shall we justify one wrong by another? This is a sufficient answer. Shall we at this moment justify the deprivation of the Negro of the right to vote, because some one else is deprived of that privilege? I hold that women, as well as men, have the right to vote, and my heart and my voice go with the movement to extend suffrage to woman; but that question rests upon another basis than that on which our right rests. We may be asked, I say, why we want it. I will tell you why we want it. We want it because it is our *right*, first of all. No class of men can, without insulting their own nature, be content with any deprivation of their rights. We want it again, as a means for educating our race. Men are so constituted that they derive their conviction of their own possibilities largely from the estimate formed of them by others. If nothing is expected of a people, that people will find it difficult to contradict that expectation. By depriving us of suffrage, you affirm our incapacity to form an intelligent judgment respecting public men and public measures; you declare before the world that we are unfit to exercise the elective franchise, and by this means lead us to undervalue ourselves, to put a low estimate upon ourselves, and to feel that we have no possibilities like other men. Again, I want the elective franchise, for one, as a colored man, because ours is a peculiar government, based upon a peculiar idea, and that idea is universal suffrage. If I were in a monarchial government, or an autocratic or aristocratic government, where the few bore rule and the many were subject, there would be no special stigma resting upon me, because I did not exercise the elective franchise. It would do me no great violence. Mingling with the mass I should partake of the strength of the mass; I should be supported by the mass, and I should have the same incentives to endeavor with the mass of my fellowmen; it would be no particular burden, no particular deprivation; but here where universal suffrage is the rule, where that is the fundamental idea of the Government, to rule us out is to make us an exception, to brand us with the stigma of inferiority, and to invite to our heads the missiles of those about us; therefore, I want the franchise for the black man.

Problems in the South

There are, however, other reasons, not derived from any consideration merely of our rights, but arising out of the conditions of the South, and of the country—considerations which have already been referred to by Mr. [Wendell] Phillips—considerations which must arrest the attention of statesmen. I believe that when the tall heads of this Rebellion shall have been swept down, as they will be swept down, when the Davises and Toombses and Stephenses, and others who are leading this rebellion shall have been blotted out, there will be this rank undergrowth of treason, to which reference has been made, growing up there, and interfering with, and thwarting the quiet operation of the Federal Government in those States. You will see those traitors, handing down, from sire to son, the same ma-

The Thirteenth and Fourteenth Amendments

In December 1865, several months after the Civil War ended, the Thirteenth Amendment, outlawing slavery in the United States, was ratified by the required three-fourths of the states and became a part of the Constitution. The Fourteenth Amendment, which made citizens of former slaves and guaranteed all Americans equal protection of the laws, was enacted in 1868. The key sections of both amendments are presented below.

Amendment XIII

Section 1. Neither slavery nor involuntary servitude, except as a punishment for crime whereof the party shall have been duly convicted, shall exist within the United States, or any place subject to their jurisdiction.

Amendment XIV

Section 1. All persons born or naturalized in the United States, and subject to the jurisdiction thereof, are citizens of the United States and of the State wherein they reside. No State shall make or enforce any law which shall abridge the privileges or immunities of citizens of the United States; nor shall any State deprive any person of life, liberty, or property, without due process of law; nor deny to any person within its jurisdiction the equal protection of the laws.

Eric Foner and John A. Garraty, *The Reader's Companion to American History.* Boston: Houghton Mifflin, 1991, p. 1,199.

lignant spirit which they have manifested, and which they are now exhibiting, with malicious hearts, broad blades, and bloody hands in the field, against our sons and brothers. That spirit will still remain; and whoever sees the Federal Government extended over those Southern States will see that Government in a strange land, and not only in a strange land, but in an enemy's land. A post-master of the United States in the South will find himself surrounded by a hostile spirit; a collector in the Southern port will find himself surrounded by a hostile spirit; a United States marshal or United States judge will be surrounded there by a hostile element. The enmity will not die out in a year, will not die out in an age. The Federal Government will be looked upon in those States precisely as the Governments of Austria and France are looked upon in Italy at the present moment. They will endeavor to circumvent, they will endeavor to destroy, the peaceful operation of this Government. Now, where will you find the strength to counterbalance this spirit, if you do not find it in the Negroes of the South? They are your friends, and have always been your friends. They were your friends even when the Government did not regard them as such. They comprehended the genius of this war before you did. It is a significant fact, it is a marvellous fact, it seems almost to imply a direct interposition of Providence, that this war, which began in the interest of slavery on both sides, bids fair to end in the interest of liberty on both sides. It was begun, I say, in the interest of slavery on both sides. The South was fighting to take slavery out of the Union, and the North fighting to keep it in the Union; the South fighting to get it beyond the limits of the United States Constitution, and the North fighting to retain it within those limits; the South fighting for new guarantees, and the North fighting for the old guarantees;— both despising the Negro, both insulting the Negro. Yet, the Negro, apparently endowed with wisdom from on high, saw more clearly the end from the beginning than we did. When [William] Seward said the status of no man in the country would be changed by the war, the Negro did not believe him. When our generals sent their underlings in shoulder-straps to hunt the flying Negro back from our lines into the jaws of slavery, from which he had escaped, the Negroes thought that a mistake had been made, and that the intentions of the Government had not been rightly understood by our officers in shoulder-straps, and they continued to come into our lines, threading their way through bogs and fens, over briers and thorns, fording streams, swimming rivers, bringing us tidings as to the safe path to march, and pointing out the dangers that threatened us. They are our only friends in the South, and we should be true to them in this their trial hour, and see to it that they have the elective franchise.

A Legacy of Inferiority

I know that we are inferior to you in some things—virtually inferior. We walk about among you like dwarfs among giants. Our heads are scarcely seen above the great sea of humanity. The Germans are superior to us; the Irish are superior to us; the Yankees are superior to us; they can do what we cannot, that is, what we have not hitherto been allowed to do. But while I make this admission, I utterly deny, that we are originally, or naturally, or practically, or in any way, or in any important sense, inferior to anybody on this globe. This charge of inferiority is an old dodge. It has been made available for oppression on many occasions. It is only about six centuries since the blue-eyed and fair-haired Anglo-Saxons were considered inferior by the haughty Normans, who once trampled upon them. If you read the history of the Norman Conquest, you will find that this proud Anglo-Saxon was once looked upon as of coarser clay than his Norman master, and might be found in the highways and byways of old England laboring with a brass collar on his neck, and the name of the master marked upon it. *You* were down then! You are up now. I am glad you are up, and I want you to be glad to help us up also.

The story of our inferiority is an old dodge, as I have said; for wherever men oppress their fellows, wherever they enslave them, they will endeavor to find the needed apology for such enslavement and oppression in the character of the people oppressed and enslaved. When we wanted, a few years ago, a slice of Mexico, it was hinted that the Mexicans were an inferior race, that the old Castilian blood had become so weak that it would scarcely run down hill, and that Mexico needed the long, strong and beneficent arm of the Anglo-Saxon care extended over it. We said that it was necessary to its salvation, and a part of the "manifest destiny" of this Republic, to extend our arm over that dilapidated government. So, too, when Russia wanted to take possession of a part of the Ottoman Empire, the Turks were "an inferior race." So, too, when England wants to set the heel of her power more firmly in the quivering heart of old Ireland, the Celts are an "inferior race." So, too, the Negro, when he is to be robbed of any right which is justly his, is an "inferior man." It is said that we are ignorant; I admit it. But if we know enough to be hung, we know enough to vote. If the Negro knows enough to pay taxes to support the government, he knows enough to vote; taxation and representation should go together. If he knows enough to shoulder a musket and fight for the flag, fight for the government, he knows enough to vote. If he knows as much when he is sober as an Irishman knows when drunk, he knows enough to vote, on good American principles.

BLACK MEN HAVE DEFENDED THE UNION

But I was saying that you needed a counterpoise in the persons of the slaves to the enmity that would exist at the South after the Rebellion is put down. I hold that the American people are bound, not only in self defence, to extend this right to the freedmen of the South, but they are bound by their love of country, and by all their regard for the future safety of those Southern States, to do this—to do it as a measure essential to the preservation of peace there. But I will now dwell upon this. I put it to the American sense of honor. The honor of a nation is an important thing. It is said in the Scriptures, "What doth it profit a man if he gain the whole world, and lose his own soul?" It may be said, also, What doth it profit a nation if it gain the whole world, but lose its honor? I hold that the American government has taken upon itself a solemn obligation of honor, to see that this war—let it be long or let it be short, let it cost much or let it cost little—that this war shall not cease until every freedman at the South has the right to vote. It has bound itself to it. What have you asked the black men of the South, the black men of the whole country, to do? Why, you have asked them to incur the deadly enmity of their masters, in order to befriend you and to befriend this Government. You have asked us to call down, not only upon ourselves, but upon our children's children, the deadly hate of the entire Southern people. You have called upon us to turn our backs upon our masters, to abandon their cause and espouse yours; to turn against the South and in favor of the North; to shoot down the Confederacy and uphold the flag—the American flag. You have called upon us to expose ourselves to all the subtle machinations of their malignity for all time. And now, what do you propose to do when you come to make peace? To reward your enemies, and trample in the dust your friends? Do you intend to sacrifice the very men who have come to the rescue of your banner in the South, and incurred the lasting displeasure of their masters thereby? Do you intend to sacrifice them and reward your enemies? Do you mean to give your enemies the right to vote, your enemies the right to vote, and take it away from your friends? Is that wise policy? Is that honorable? Could American honor withstand such a blow? I do not believe you will do it. I think you will see to it that we have the right to vote. There is something too mean in looking upon the Negro, when you are in trouble, as a citizen, and when you are free from trouble, as an alien. When this nation was in trouble, in its early struggles, it looked upon the Negro as a citizen. In 1776 he was a citizen. At the time of the formation of the Constitution the Negro had the right to vote in eleven States out of the old thirteen. In your trouble you have made us citizens. In 1812 Gen. [Andrew] Jackson addressed us as citizens—"fellow-citizens." He wanted us to fight. We were citi-

Frederick Douglass

zens then! And now, when you come to frame a conscription bill, the Negro is a citizen again. He has been a citizen just three times in the history of this government, and it has always been in time of trouble. In time of trouble we are citizens. Shall we be citizens in war, and aliens in peace? Would that be just?

LEAVE THE NEGRO ALONE

I ask my friends who are apologizing for not insisting upon this right, where can the black man look, in this country, for the assertion of his right, if he may not look to the Massachusetts Anti-Slavery Society? Where under the whole heavens can he look for sympathy, in asserting this right, if he may not look to this platform? Have you lifted us up to a certain height to see that we are men, and then are any disposed to leave us there, without seeing that we are put in possession of all our rights? We look naturally to this platform for the assertion of all our rights, and for this one especially. I understand the anti-slavery societies of this country to be based on two principles,—first, the freedom of the blacks of this country; and, second, the elevation of them. Let me not be misunderstood here. I am not asking for sympathy at the hands of abolitionists, sympathy at the hands of any. I think the American people are disposed often to be generous rather than just. I look over this country at the present time, and I see Educational Societies, Sanitary Commissions, Freedmen's Associations, and the like,—all very good: but in regard to the colored people there is always more that is benevolent, I perceive, than just, manifested towards us. What I ask for the Negro is not benevolence, not pity, not sympathy, but simply *justice*. The American people have always been anxious to know what they shall do with us. Gen. [Nathaniel] Banks was distressed with solicitude as to what he should do with the Negro. Everybody has asked the question, and they learned to ask it early of the abolitionists, "What shall we do with the Negro?" I have had but one answer from the beginning. Do nothing with us! Your doing with us has already played the mischief with us. Do nothing with us! If the apples will not remain on the tree of their own strength, if they are worm-eaten at the core, if they are early ripe and disposed to fall, let them fall! I am not for tying or fastening them on the tree in any way, except by nature's plan, and if they will not stay there, let them fall. And if the Negro cannot stand on his own legs, let him fall alone! If you see him on his way to school, let him alone, don't disturb him! If you see him going to the dinner-table at a hotel, let him go! If you see him going to the ballot-box, let him alone, don't disturb him! If you see him going into a work-shop, just let him alone,—your interference is doing him a positive injury. Gen. Banks' "preparation" is of a piece with this attempt to prop up the Negro. Let him fall if he cannot stand alone! If the Negro cannot live by the line of eternal justice, so beautifully pictured to you in the illustration used by Mr. Phillips, the fault will not be yours, it will be his who made the Negro, and established that line for his government. Let him live or die by that. If you will only untie his hands, and give him a chance, I think he will live. He will work as readily for himself as the white man. A great many delusions have been swept away by this war. One was, that the Negro would not work; he has proved his ability to work. Another was, that the Negro would not fight; that he possessed only the most sheepish attributes of humanity; was a perfect lamb, or an "Uncle Tom"; disposed to take off his coat whenever required, fold his hands, and be whipped by anybody who wanted to whip him. But the war has proved that there is a great deal of human nature in the Negro, and that "he will fight," as Mr. [Edmund] Quincy, our President, said, in earlier days than these, "when there is a reasonable probability of his whipping anybody."

The Emergence of Black Politics During Reconstruction

ERIC FONER

Eric Foner, a distinguished American historian who teaches at Columbia University, is the author of several books on the Civil War era, including *Free Soil, Free Labor, Free Men: The Ideology of the Republican Party Before the Civil War* and *Reconstruction: America's Unfinished Revolution, 1863–1877.* In this selection, which is excerpted from his book *Reconstruction,* Foner discusses the development of black politics in the South following the Civil War. According to Foner, African American political leaders emerged in the South immediately after the war. The central concerns of these leaders were voting rights and equality before the law—to bring to former slaves the full rights of citizenship.

I f the goal of autonomy inspired blacks to withdraw from religious and social institutions controlled by whites and to attempt to work out their economic destinies for themselves, in the polity, "freedom" meant inclusion rather than separation. Recognition of their equal rights as citizens quickly emerged as the animating impulse of Reconstruction black politics. In the spring and summer of 1865, blacks organized a seemingly unending series of mass meetings, parades, and petitions demanding civil equality and the suffrage as indispensable corollaries of emancipation. The most extensive mobilization occurred in areas that had been occupied by Union troops during the war, where political activity had begun even before 1865. Union Leagues and similar groups sprang up in low country South Carolina and Georgia, their meetings bringing together

Freedmen's Bureau agents, black soldiers, and local freedmen, to demand the vote and the repeal of all laws discriminating against blacks. "By the Declaration of Independence," declared a gathering on St. Helena Island, "we believe these are rights which cannot justly be denied us."

MOBILIZING IN THE SOUTH

Political mobilization also proceeded apace in Southern cities, where the flourishing network of churches and fraternal societies provided a springboard for organization, and the army and Freedmen's Bureau stood ready to offer protection. In Wilmington, North Carolina, freedmen in 1865 formed an Equal Rights League which, local officials reported, insisted upon "all the social and political rights of white citizens" and demanded that blacks be consulted in the selection of policemen, justices of the peace, and county commissioners. By midsummer, "secret political Radical Associations" had been formed in Virginia's major cities. Richmond blacks first organized politically to protest the army's rounding up of "vagrants" for plantation labor, but soon expanded their demands to include the right to vote and the removal of the "Rebel-controlled" local government. In Norfolk, occupied by the Union Army since 1862, blacks early in 1865 created the Union Monitor Club to press their claim to equal rights, and in May hundreds attempted to vote in a local election. A mass meeting endorsed a militant statement drafted by former fugitive slave Thomas Bayne: "Traitors shall not dictate or prescribe to us the terms or conditions of our citizenship."

In Louisiana, where black politics had advanced furthest during the war, the New Orleans *Tribune* and its Radical allies continued to press the issue of black suffrage. A September 1865 convention composed of native white Radicals, Northerners like the young provost judge and future governor Henry C. Warmoth, and prominent members of the free black elite, voted to affiliate with the national Republican Party, called upon Congress to govern Louisiana as a territory, and demanded full legal and political equality for blacks. Meanwhile, mobilization penetrated the sugar country, with laborers, one planter complained, abandoning work at will to attend political gatherings. In November, as white Louisianans went to the polls, a Republican-sponsored "voluntary election" attracted some 20,000 voters, mostly blacks in New Orleans and the surrounding parishes, who "elected" Warmoth to serve as Louisiana's "Territorial delegate" to Congress. "The whole Parish was in an uproar" on election day, reported an army officer, with hundreds of freedmen abandoning the plantations, "stating that they were going to vote."

Statewide conventions held throughout the South in 1865 and early 1866 offered the most visible evidence of black political organization. Several hundred delegates attended these gatherings, some selected by local meetings occasionally marked by "animated debate," others by churches, fraternal societies, Union Leagues, and black army units, still others simply appointed by themselves. "Some bring credentials," observed North Carolina black leader James H. Harris, "others had as much as they could do to bring themselves, having to escape from their homes stealthily at night" to avoid white reprisal. Although little information survives about the majority of these individuals, certain patterns can be discerned from the fragmentary evidence. The delegates "ranged all colors and apparently all conditions," but urban free mulattoes took the most prominent roles, and former slaves were almost entirely absent from leadership positions. One speaker at the Tennessee gathering doubted it should be called a "Negro convention" at all, since its officers were "all mixed blood," some "as white as the editor of the New York *Herald*." Charleston free blacks, along with six Northern-born newcomers, dominated South Carolina's gathering, and at Louisiana's Republican state convention nineteen of the twenty black delegates had been born free. But other groups also came to the fore in 1865. In Mississippi, a state with few free blacks before the war, ex-slave army veterans and their relatives comprised the majority of the delegates. Alabama and Georgia had a heavy representation of black ministers, and all the conventions included numerous skilled artisans. Many of the delegates, especially those born free, were relatively well-to-do, although the very richest blacks held aloof, too linked to whites economically and by kinship to risk taking an active role in politics.

PROMINENT BLACK LEADERS

The prominence of free blacks, ministers, artisans, and former soldiers in these early conventions established patterns that would characterize black politics for much of Reconstruction. From among these delegates would emerge such prominent officeholders as Alabama Congressman James T. Rapier and Mississippi Secretary of State James D. Lynch. The most remarkable continuity in black leadership occurred in South Carolina, for among the fifty-two delegates to the November 1865 convention sat four future Congressmen, thirteen legislators, and twelve delegates to the state's 1868 constitutional convention. In general, however, what is striking is how few of these early leaders went on to positions of prominence. Only two of Alabama's fifty-six delegates (William V. Turner and Holland Thompson) later played significant roles in Reconstruction politics, a pattern repeated in Virginia, North Carolina, Tennessee, Mississippi, Alabama, and Arkansas. In most states, black political mobilization had advanced far more rapidly in cities and in rural areas occupied by federal troops during the war, than in the bulk of the plantation counties, where the majority of the former slaves lived. The free blacks of Louisiana and South Carolina who stepped to the fore in 1865 would remain at the helm of black politics throughout Reconstruction; nowhere, however, a new group of leaders, many of them freedmen from the black belt, would soon supersede those who had taken the lead in 1865.

The debates at these conventions illuminated conflicting currents of black public life in the immediate aftermath of emancipation. Tensions within the black community occasionally rose to the surface. One delegate remarked that he did not intend "to have the whip of slavery cracked over us by no slaveholder's son"; another voiced resentment that a Northerner (Pennsylvania-born

James W. Hood) had been chosen president of North Carolina's convention; and the printed proceedings of the South Carolina convention included a discreet reference to the "spirited discussion" produced by a resolution referring to blacks' making "distinctions among ourselves." Relations between the races caused debate as well. A resolution urging blacks to employ, wherever possible, teachers of their own race, was tabled by the North Carolina delegates after considerable debate, and replaced by one thanking Northern societies for their efforts on behalf of the freedmen. By and large, however, the proceedings proved harmonious, the delegates devoting most of their time to issues that united blacks rather than dividing them. South Carolina's convention demanded the full gamut of opportunities and privileges enjoyed by whites, from access to education to the right to bear arms, serve on juries, establish newspapers, assemble peacefully, "enter upon all the avenues of agriculture, commerce, [and] trade," and "develop our whole being by all the appliances that belong to civilized society." Georgia's resolutions complained of violence inflicted on rural blacks, efforts to prevent freedmen from establishing schools, and attempts to keep from blacks the church property "paid for by our own earnings while we were in slavery."

EQUALITY AND SUFFRAGE

The delegates' central preoccupation, however, was equality before the law and the suffrage. A number of New Orleans and Charleston free blacks, to be sure, still flirted with the idea of confining black suffrage to a privileged minority through some combination of property and educational qualifications, although they insisted that such requirements apply to both races. ("If the ignorant white man is allowed to vote," declared a petition of prominent Charleston free blacks, the "ignorant colored man" should be enfranchised as well.) Yet at the 1865 conventions speaker after speaker echoed the view that universal manhood suffrage constituted "an essential and inseparable element of self-government." In justifying their demand for the vote, the delegates invoked America's republican traditions, especially the Declaration of Independence, "the broadest, the deepest, the most comprehensive and truthful definition of human freedom that was ever given to the world." "The colored people," Hood would declare in 1868, "had read the Declaration until it had become part of their natures." The North Carolina freedmen's convention he chaired in 1865 portrayed the Civil War and emancipation as chapters in the onward march of "progressive civilization," embodiments of "the fundamental truths laid down in the great charter of Republican liberty, the Declaration of Independence." Such language was not confined to the convention delegates. Eleven Alabama blacks, who complained of contract frauds, injustice before the courts, and other abuses, concluded their petition with a revealing masterpiece of understatement: "This is not the persuit of happiness."

There was more here than merely familiar wording. Like Northern blacks steeped in the Great Tradition of prewar protest, the freedmen and Southern free blacks saw emancipation as enabling the nation to live up to the full implications of its republican creed—a goal that could be achieved only by abandoning racial proscription and absorbing blacks fully into the civil and political order. Isham Sweat, a slave-born barber who wrote the address of North Carolina's convention and went on to serve in the state legislature, told John R. Dennett that Congress should "declare that no state had a republican form of government if every free man in it was not equal before the law." Another 1865 speaker destined for Reconstruction prominence, Louisiana's Oscar J. Dunn, described the absence of "discrimination among men" and "hereditary distinctions" as the essence of America's political heritage. Continued proscription of blacks, Dunn warned, would jeopardize the republic's very future, opening "the door for the institution of aristocracy, nobility, and even monarchy."

Like their Northern counterparts during the Civil War, Southern blacks proclaimed their identification with the nation's history, destiny, and political system. The very abundance of letters and petitions addressed by black gatherings and ordinary freedmen to officials of the army, Freedmen's Bureau, and state and federal authorities, as well as the decision of a number of conventions to send representatives to Washington to lobby for black rights, revealed a belief that the political order was at least partially open to their influence. "We are Americans," declared a meeting of Norfolk blacks, "we know no other country, we love the land of our birth." Their address reminded white Virginians that in 1619, "our fathers as well as yours were toiling in the plantations on James River" and that a black man, Crispus Attucks, had shed "the first blood" in the American Revolution. And, of course, blacks had fought and died to save the Union. America, resolved another Virginia meeting, was "now *our* country—made emphatically so by the blood of our brethren." "We stood by the government when it wanted help," a delegate to Mississippi's convention wrote President [Andrew] Johnson. "Now ... will it stand by us?"

A MODERATE AND CAUTIOUS TONE

Despite the insistent language of individual speeches, the convention resolutions and public addresses adopted a moderate tone, offering "the right hand of fellowship" to Southern whites. The Virginia convention proved an exception, for its address spoke of "injuries deeper and darker than the earth ever witnessed in the case of any other people." At one point, the Virginia delegates changed the wording of a public statement from "our former masters" to "our former oppressors." Elsewhere, however, a far more conciliatory approach prevailed. Leaders of North Carolina's convention advocated "equal rights, and a moderate conservative course in demanding them." One rural delegate who proposed that the assembly demand admission to the state's constitutional convention, then in session in Raleigh, was denounced as "absurd and foolish," and the gathering "respectfully and humbly" petitioned the state government for education and equality before the law, while avoiding reference to the suffrage. Georgia's delegates, divided between advocates of universal suffrage and those favoring a literacy or property test, compromised by claiming "at least conditional suffrage." Even the South Carolina convention, forthright in claiming civil and political equality and in identifying its demands with "the cause of millions of oppressed men" throughout the world, took pains to assure the state's white minority of blacks' "spirit of meekness," their consciousness of "your wealth and greatness, and our poverty and weakness."

To some extent, this cautious tone reflected a realistic assessment of the political situation at a time when Southern whites had been restored to local power by President Johnson, and Congress had not yet launched its own Reconstruction policy. But the conventions' mixture of radicalism and conciliation also mirrored the indecision of an emerging class of black political leaders still finding their own voice in 1865 and 1866, and dominated by urban free blacks, ministers, and others who had in the past enjoyed harmonious relations with at least some local whites and did not always feel the bitter resentments of rural freedmen.

INDECISION AMONG BLACK LEADERS

Nor did a coherent economic program emerge from these assemblies. Demands for land did surface at local meetings that chose convention delegates. One such gathering in Greensboro, Alabama, heard speakers call for "land or blood," while at Tarboro, North Carolina, where two candidates presented themselves to 1,500 blacks, the one who called for a division of the land was unanimously elected. Yet such views rarely found expression among the conventions' leadership. Virginia's delegates pointedly observed that the Freedmen's Bureau Act had promised blacks access to land, Georgia's petitioned Congress to validate the Sherman land grants, and South Carolina's requested Congress to place "a fair and impartial construction" upon the "pledges of government to us concerning the land question." But by and large, economic concerns figured only marginally in the proceedings, and the addresses and resolutions offered no economic program, apart from stressing the "mutual interest" of capital and labor, and urging self-improvement as the route to personal advancement. The Arkansas resolutions even remarked that blacks "are destined in the future, as in the past, to cultivate your cotton fields." A number of conventions chided idle freedmen for "vagrancy and pauperism," and urged them to remain on the land, labor diligently, and save money in order to purchase homesteads.

Thus, the ferment rippling through the Southern country-side found little echo at the state conventions of 1865—a re-flection of the paucity of representation from the plantation counties and the prominence of political leaders more attuned to political equality and self-help formulas than to rural freed-men's thirst for land. Nor did the conventions' eloquent appeals for civil and political equality accomplish anything, for all were ignored by the intransigent state governments of Presidential Reconstruction. As a result, enthusiasm for such gatherings waned. Among the states of the Confederacy, only Georgia, Tennessee, North Carolina, and Texas witnessed black conven-tions in 1866. One delegate noted that his constituents believed "we do nothing but meet, pass resolutions, publish pamphlets, and incur expenses, without accomplishing good results."

While understandable, this indictment was perhaps unfair, for these early black conventions both reflected and advanced the process of political mobilization. Some Tennessee delegates, for example, took to heart their convention's instruction to "look after the welfare" of their constituents. After returning home, they actively promoted black education, protested to civil au-thorities and the Freedmen's Bureau about violence and con-tract frauds, and struggled against unequal odds to secure blacks a modicum of justice in local courts. Chapters of the Georgia Equal Rights and Educational Association, established at the state's January 1866 convention, became "schools in which the colored citizens learn their rights." Spreading into fifty counties by the end of the year, the association's local meetings attracted as many as 2,000 freedmen, who listened to speeches on issues of the day and readings from Republican newspapers. And, al-though plagued by financial problems and the difficulty of reaching an overwhelmingly illiterate audience, the emerging black press also promoted the spread of political education. By 1866, nine (mostly short-lived) black newspapers had joined the

New Orleans *Tribune*. Edited by two white Northerners, but owned and managed by a black board of directors, the Mobile *Nationalist* sent agents into the countryside to solicit subscriptions, report on local conditions, and urge freedmen "to stand up like men on behalf of [their] rights." Blacks able to read the *Nationalist*, one Alabama white complained, absorbed "the 'radicalism' it contains," became "*pugnacious*," and no longer exhibited proper respect for their former owners.

AN ONGOING PROCESS OF POLITICIZATION

Although few in number, the statewide conventions of 1866 illustrated the results of this ongoing process of politicization. Twice as many counties were represented in the Georgia and North Carolina gatherings as the year before, reflecting how organization had penetrated the black belt. In Greene County, North Carolina, unrepresented at the first state convention, blacks in 1866 held an election to choose a delegate from between two candidates who conducted "a regular canvass." Former slaves now began to assume positions of prominence monopolized by the freeborn a year earlier, and the resolutions and speeches were noticeably more radical. North Carolina's delegates heard militant speeches chastising whites for violence against freedmen, injustice to black laborers, and opposition to black education. Their resolutions demanded equal suffrage (an issue sidestepped in 1865), praised Charles Sumner, Thaddeus Stevens, and other Radical Republicans as "beacon lights of our race," and urged blacks to combat economic inequalities by forming joint stock companies and patronizing, wherever possible, businessmen of their own race. The Tennessee convention called upon Congress to grant the state "a republican form of government" under which blacks could vote, bear arms, and educate their children. But even more striking than this new tone was the wholesale turnover in membership. Only a small minority of the 1865 delegates (seventeen of 106 in North Carolina, eighteen of 102 in Tennessee) reappeared in 1866. Even in South Carolina, with its continuity in black political leadership, Richard H. Cain observed that some early leaders, including prominent free blacks, had by 1866 "relapsed into secondary men; and the class who were hardly known" were stepping forward to assume prominent roles.

All in all, the most striking characteristic of this initial phase of black political mobilization was its very unevenness. In some states, organization proceeded steadily in 1865 and 1866, in others, such as Mississippi, little activity occurred between an initial flurry in the summer of 1865 and the advent of black suffrage two years later. Large parts of the black belt remained untouched by organized politics, but many blacks were aware of Congressional debates on Reconstruction policy, and quickly employed on their own behalf the Civil Rights Act of 1866. "The negro of today," remarked a correspondent of the New Orleans *Tribune* in September 1866, "is not the same as he was six years ago.... He has been told of his rights, which have long been robbed." Only in 1867 would blacks enter the "political nation," but in organization, leadership, and an ideology that drew upon America's republican heritage to demand an equal place as citizens, the seeds that flowered then were planted in the first years of freedom.

The Civil Rights Act of 1866

U.S. CONGRESS

Immediately after the Civil War, the U.S. Congress, dominated by Republicans, acted to extend citizenship rights to the slaves who were set free by the Emancipation Proclamation and Thirteenth Amendment to the Constitution. The Civil Rights Act of 1866 was passed by Congress but vetoed by President Andrew Johnson. Congress overrode the president's veto, making the Civil Rights Act of 1866 the first piece of civil rights legislation passed during the Reconstruction era. The bill made citizens of all persons born in the United States, regardless of race or previous condition of servitude. Two years after the passage of this law, Congress acted again to include these basic citizenship rights in the Constitution in the Fourteenth Amendment.

*B*e it enacted by the Senate and House of Representatives of the United States of America in Congress assembled, That all persons born in the United States and not subject to any foreign power, excluding Indians not taxed, are hereby declared to be citizens of the United States; and such citizens, of every race and color, without regard to any previous condition of slavery or involuntary servitude, except as a punishment for crime whereof the party shall have been duly convicted, shall have the same right, in every State and Territory in the United States, to make and enforce contracts, to sue, be parties, and give evidence, to inherit, purchase, lease, sell, hold, and convey real and personal property, and to full and equal benefit of all laws and proceedings for the security of person and property, as is enjoyed by white citizens, and shall be subject to like punishment, pains, and penalties, and to none other, any law, statute, ordinance, reg-

U.S. Congress, *United States Statutes at Large, XIV.* 39th Congress, 1st–2nd Sessions, 1865–67.

ulation, or custom, to the contrary notwithstanding.

SECTION 2. *And be it further enacted*, That any person who, under color of any law, statute, ordinance, regulation, or custom, shall subject, or cause to be subjected, any inhabitant of any State or Territory to the deprivation of any right secured or protected by this act, or to different punishment, pains, or penalties on account of such person having at any time been held in a condition of slavery or involuntary servitude, except as a punishment for crime whereof the party shall have been duly convicted, or by reason of his color or race, than is prescribed for the punishment of white persons, shall be deemed guilty of a misdemeanor, and, on conviction, shall be punished by fine not exceeding one thousand dollars, or imprisonment not exceeding one year, or both, in the discretion of the court.

PROTECTION FROM THE COURTS

SECTION 3. *And be it further enacted*, That the district courts of the United States, within their respective districts, shall have, exclusively of the courts of the several States, cognizance of all crimes and offences committed against the provisions of this act, and also, concurrently with the circuit courts of the United States, of all causes, civil and criminal, affecting persons who are denied or cannot enforce in the courts or judicial tribunals of the State or locality where they may be any of the rights secured to them by the first section of this act; and if any suit or prosecution, civil or criminal, has been or shall be commenced in any State court, against any such person, for any cause whatsoever, or against any officer civil or military, or other person, for any arrest or imprisonment, trespasses, or wrongs done or committed by virtue or under color of authority derived from this act or the act establishing a Bureau for the relief of Freedmen and Refugees, and all acts amendatory thereof, or for refusing to do any act upon the ground that it would be inconsistent with this act, such defendant shall have the right to remove such cause for trial to the proper district or circuit court in the manner prescribed by the "Act relating to habeas corpus and regulating judicial proceedings in certain cases," approved March three, eighteen hundred and sixty-three, and all acts amendatory thereof. The jurisdiction in civil and criminal matters hereby conferred on the district and circuit courts of the United States shall be exercised and enforced in conformity with the laws of the United States, so far as such laws are suitable to carry the same into effect; but in all cases where such laws are not adapted to the object, or are deficient in the provisions necessary to furnish suitable remedies and punish offences against law, the common law, as modified and changed by the constitution and statutes of the State wherein the court having jurisdiction of the cause, civil or criminal, is held, so far as the same is not inconsistent with the Constitution and laws of the United States, shall be extended to and govern said courts in the trial and disposition of such cause, and, if of a criminal nature, in the infliction of punishment on the party found guilty.

ENFORCEMENT OF THIS ACT

SECTION 4. *And be it further enacted*, That the district attorneys, marshals, and deputy marshals of the United States, the commissioners appointed by the circuit and territorial courts of the United States, with powers of arresting, imprisoning, or bailing offenders against the laws of the United States, the officers and agents of the Freedmen's Bureau, and every other officer who may be specially empowered by the President of the United States, shall be, and they are hereby, specially authorized and required, at the expense of the United States, to institute proceedings against all and every person who shall violate the provisions of this act, and cause him or them to be arrested and imprisoned, or bailed, as the case may be, for trial before such court of the United States or territorial court as by this act has cognizance of the offence. And with a view to affording reasonable protection to all persons in their constitutional rights of equality before the law, without distinction of race or color, or previous condition of slavery or involuntary servitude, except as a punishment for crime, whereof the party shall have been duly convicted, and to the prompt discharge of the duties of this act, it shall be the duty of the circuit courts of the United

States and the superior courts of the Territories of the United States, from time to time, to increase the number of commissioners, so as to afford a speedy and convenient means for the arrest and examination of persons charged with a violation of this act; and such commissioners are hereby authorized and required to exercise and discharge all the powers and duties conferred on them by this act, and the same duties with regard to offences created by this act, as they are authorized by law to exercise with regard to other offences against the laws of the United States.

SECTION 5. *And be it further enacted,* That it shall be the duty of all marshals and deputy marshals to obey and execute all warrants and precepts issued under the provisions of this act, when to them directed; and should any marshal or deputy marshal refuse to receive such warrant or other process when tendered, or to use all proper means diligently to execute the same, he shall, on conviction thereof, he fined in the sum of one thousand dollars, to the use of the person upon whom the accused is alleged to have committed the offence. And the better to enable the said commissioners to execute their duties faithfully and efficiently, in conformity with the Constitution of the United States and the requirements of this act, they are hereby authorized and empowered, within their counties respectively, to appoint, in writing, under their hands, any one or more suitable persons, from time to time, to execute all such warrants and other process as may be issued by them in the lawful performance of their respective duties; and the persons so appointed to execute any warrant or process as aforesaid shall have authority to summon and call to their aid the bystanders or posse comitatus of the proper county, or such portion of the land or naval forces of the United States, or of the militia, as may be necessary to the performance of the duty with which they are charged, and to insure a faithful observance of the clause of the Constitution which prohibits slavery, in conformity with the provisions of this act; and said warrants shall run and be executed by said officers anywhere in the State or Territory within which they are issued.

SECTION 6. *And be it further enacted*, That any person who shall knowingly and wilfully obstruct, hinder, or prevent any officer, or other person charged with the execution of any warrant or process issued under the provisions of this act, or any person or persons lawfully assisting him or them, from arresting any person for whose apprehension such warrant or process may have been issued, or shall rescue or attempt to rescue such person from the custody of the officer, other person or persons, or those lawfully assisting as aforesaid, when so arrested pursuant to the authority herein given and declared, or shall aid, abet, or assist any person so arrested as aforesaid, directly or indirectly, to escape from the custody of the officer or other person legally authorized as aforesaid, or shall harbor or conceal any person for whose arrest a warrant or process shall have been issued as aforesaid, so as to prevent his discovery and arrest after notice or knowledge of the fact that a warrant has been issued for the apprehension of such person, shall, for either of said offences, be subject to a fine not exceeding one thousand dollars, and imprisonment not exceeding six months, by indictment and conviction before the district court of the United States for the district in which said offence may have been committed, or before the proper court of criminal jurisdiction, if committed within any one of the organized Territories of the United States.

SECTION 7. *And be it further enacted*, That the district attorneys, the marshals, their deputies, and the clerks of the said district and territorial courts shall be paid for their services the like fees as may be allowed to them for similar services in other cases; and in all cases where the proceedings are before a commissioner, he shall be entitled to a fee of ten dollars in full for his services in each case, inclusive of all services incident to such arrest and examination. The person or persons authorized to execute the process to be issued by such commissioners for the arrest of offenders against the provisions of this act shall be entitled to a fee of five dollars for each person he or they may arrest and take before any such commissioner as aforesaid, with such other fees as may be deemed reasonable by such commissioner for such other additional services as may be necessarily performed by him or them, such as attending at the examination, keeping the prisoner in custody, and providing him with food and lodging during his detention, and until the final determination of such commissioner, and in general for performing such other duties as may be required in the premises; such fees to be made up in conformity with the fees usually charged by the officers of the courts of justice within the proper district or county, as near as may be practicable, and paid out of the Treasury of the United States on the certificate of the judge of the district within which the arrest is made, and to be recoverable from the defendant as part of the judgment in case of conviction.

THE ROLE OF THE PRESIDENT

SECTION 8. *And be it further enacted*, That whenever the President of the United States shall have reason to believe that offences have been or are likely to be committed against the provisions of this act within any judicial district, it shall be lawful for him, in his discretion, to direct the judge, marshal, and district attorney of such district to attend at such place within the district, and for such time as he may designate, for the purpose of the more speedy arrest and trial of persons charged with a violation of this act; and it shall be the duty of every judge or other officer, when any such requisition shall be received by him, to attend at the place and for the time therein designated.

SECTION 9. *And be it further enacted*, That it shall be lawful for the President of the United States, or such person as he may empower for that purpose, to employ such part of the land or naval forces of the United States, or of the militia, as shall be necessary to prevent the violation and enforce the due execution of this act.

SECTION 10. *And be it further enacted*, That upon all questions of law arising in any cause under the provisions of this act a final appeal may be taken to the Supreme Court of the United States.

The Failure of Reconstruction

In the following viewpoint Chester J. Wynne, a scholar of Reconstruction, describes the situation faced by blacks in the post–Civil War era. Despite the passage of the Thirteenth Amendment abolishing slavery in 1865, African Americans continued to face discrimination in the United States. While many whites were committed to the ideal of equality for blacks, they feared that granting economic and political power to freed slaves would undermine their own favored status. As a result, white leaders passed oppressive laws, the courts handed down restrictive rulings, and racist violence escalated. These actions established a system of legalized segregation and denial of black civil rights that persisted until the end of the nineteenth century.

The end of slavery might have destroyed the social system of the Old South, but it did nothing to eliminate racism. As early as 1865 legislatures in all Southern states except North Carolina enacted Black Codes designed to control blacks and to restrict their civil rights. Although these regulations varied from state to state, the most common provisions included the establishment of racial segregation in public places, the prohibition of interracial marriage, and the legal recognition of marriages between blacks. Black Codes also prevented blacks from serving on juries or from testifying against whites in court, though they could give testimony against other blacks. In some states, such as Mississippi, these laws reinstituted many of the criminal provisions of the slave codes. The Mississippi law, for example, declared that "all penal and criminal laws now in force describing the mode of punishment of crimes and misdemeanors committed by slaves, free negroes, or mulattoes are hereby reenacted, and decreed to be in full force against all freedmen, free negroes, and mulattoes."

SLAVES IN EVERYTHING BUT NAME

The Black Codes in general forbade blacks from entering any but agricultural employment. In Mississippi they prevented blacks from buying or renting farmland and required them to sign an annual labor contract with a white employer; in South Carolina they made it illegal for blacks to purchase or own city lots and compelled them to pay a tax of between $10 and $100 to enter an occupation other than farming or domestic service. Blacks were also prohibited from leaving the plantation, or from entertaining guests upon it, without permission. If blacks could not give evidence of being employed, they could be detained under a charge of vagrancy and fined, or bound to work for a white landowner if unable to pay. The vagrancy statute imposed involuntary labor as punishment for a wide array of persons deemed antisocial, including:

> rogues and vagabonds, idle and dissipated persons, beggars, jugglers, or persons practicing unlawful games or plays, run-aways, common drunkards, common night-walkers, lewd, wanton, or lascivious persons, . . . common railers and brawlers, persons who neglect their calling or employment, misspend what they earn, or do not provide for the support of themselves or their families, or dependents, and all other idle and disorderly persons, including all who neglect all lawful business, habitually misspend their time by frequenting houses of ill-fame, gaming houses, or tippling shops.

Apprenticeship laws authorized the state to bind out to white employers black children whose parents could not support them or who were "not teaching them habits of industry and honesty; or are persons of notoriously bad character."

Although either the Federal Army, the Freedmen's Bureau, or the Civil Rights Act (1866) invalidated most of the Black Codes, these laws reveal what the contours of social and race relations in the post–Civil War South would have been if left entirely in the hands of whites. As African American historian W.E.B. Du Bois observed, the Black Codes represented "what the South proposed to do to the emancipated Negro, unless restrained by the nation." Black Congressman Josiah Walls warned that the Black Codes indicated what Southern Democrats would do "if they should ever again obtain control of this Government." In essence, whites intended these laws to keep blacks a propertyless, rural, laboring class, slaves in everything but name.

With the adoption of the Black Codes, the freedmen, indeed, found themselves cruelly thrust back into much the same position they had occupied as slaves. The laws that had recognized their citizenship and their rights disappeared. Some freedmen nonetheless protested their mistreatment. A letter to the governor of Mississippi from a group of freedmen asked that if "Mississippi has abolished slavery, . . . does she mean it or is it a policy for the present?" Further, they pointed out that "now we are free, we do not want to be hunted by negro runners and their hounds unless we are guilty of a criminal crime."

Most blacks sensibly realized that their protests would have little effect on the situation and might in some ways even make it worse. A writer in one African American newspaper declared that the Black Codes "express an average of the justice and humanity which the late slaveholders possess." He felt assured, though, that with the aid of the federal government "the right will prevail and truth [will] triumph in the end." For the time being, the government appeared to respond sympathetically to the plight of blacks, suspending the Black Codes in several states. Some Southern state legislatures repealed the harshest laws on their own. While the Codes were thought "dead," however, the forces that had created them were very much alive.

VIOLENCE AND TERROR

With the failure of the Black Codes, Southern whites tried to curb the freedom and power of blacks through intimidation, violence, and terror, with the largest number of violent acts arising from the attempts of blacks to assert their rights. Freedmen were assaulted and, in some cases, murdered for not satisfying their employers, for trying to buy or rent land, or for simply trying to leave the plantations on which they had once been enslaved. One Tennessee newspaper reported that white "regulators" were "riding about whipping, maiming and killing all the negroes who do not obey the orders of their former masters, just as if slavery existed." Many former black soldiers who had fought for the Union returned home only to find cinders and ashes. The rising tide of racist violence prompted one Louisiana freedman to declare: "I would say to every colored soldier, 'Bring your gun home'." Other blacks wearily realized that out of the ruin of the Civil War another conflict was smoldering. Whites knew it, too, for a former governor of North Carolina remarked "with reference to Emancipation, we are at the beginning of the war."

Perhaps the greatest threat to the freedmen was the appearance of a new organization determined to unnerve and overpower blacks and their white supporters: the Ku Klux Klan. Organized in 1866 in Pulaski, Tennessee, the Klan set out to restore white supremacy throughout the South. Klansmen rode about the Southern countryside wearing white masks and robes, issuing threats, harassing blacks, and on occasion engaging in destruction, violence, and murder. During their brief career, the Klan and similar groups such as the Knights of the White Camellia and the White League "whipped, shot, hanged, robbed, raped, and otherwise outraged Negroes and Republicans across the South in the name of preserving white civilization."

Congress struck back at the Klan with three Enforcement Acts passed in 1870 and 1871. The first of these measures made it a federal offense to interfere with any citizen's right to vote. The second placed the election of Congressmen under the supervision of federal election officials and marshals. The third, the so-called Ku Klux Klan Act, made it illegal to engage in conspiracies, to wear disguises in public, and to resist, threaten, or in any way intimidate officials of the courts or the government.

Federal mandates and prosecutions weakened the Klan, but such societies as the Mississippi Rifle Club and the South Carolina Red Shirts continued to harass blacks and white Republicans, enabling conservative whites gradually to reassume control of government and society in one Southern state after another. Republicans fell out of power in Virginia and Tennessee in 1869 and Georgia and North Carolina in 1870, even though the "Old North State" had a Republican governor until 1876. Republicans held on longer in the states of the Deep South, which had larger black populations than those in the upper South. In the elections of 1876, however, voters dismissed the Republicans from office in South Carolina, Louisiana, and Florida, the three remaining states where they held sway.

FEARS OF "NEGRO DOMINATION"

Northern support for Reconstruction (1865–1877) had begun to wane with the Panic of 1873. Economic hard times distracted Northerners from the problems of the former slaves and made Reconstruction programs seem an expensive luxury. Even whites who favored racial equality usually thought in terms of legal equality, which they believed would naturally follow from emancipation. Yet, for freedom to be meaningful and equality assured, the federal government had to guarantee the physical safety of black men and women and support their liberty by giving them land. When the government failed to do so, Reconstruction faltered and then collapsed.

For a brief period during the 1870s and 1880s greater flexibility and tolerance had characterized race relations in the South. The former slave owner, wrote a South Carolina newspaper editor, "has no desire to browbeat, maltreat, and spit upon the colored man." There lingered among many white Southerners feelings of benevolence and paternalism toward blacks, and in any event most did not regard blacks as a threat to the existing social and political order.

Such attitudes began to change in the early 1890s when the Populist, or People's, Party tried to organize black and white farmers into a political coalition to challenge for control of state governments throughout the South. "You are kept apart," Populist leader Tom Watson of Georgia told an audience of black and white farmers, "in order that you may be separately fleeced." Such language frightened those in power. They responded by appealing to the fears of Southern whites that the South would again come under "Negro domination," as they believed had been the case during Reconstruction.

DISFRANCHISEMENT OF BLACKS

Since competition for the black vote was growing, that relatively small group of men who dominated Southern politics at the end of the nineteenth century, known as the Bourbons, reasoned it was best to eliminate the black vote altogether. The Bourbons were members of the Democratic Party. As long as they could manipulate the black vote to their liking, they had no objection to blacks' going to the polls and selecting the Democratic candidate of their choice. It was, however, another matter entirely when their Republican, Independent, and especially Populist adversaries began striving to capture the black vote. Under those circumstances, the right of blacks to vote had to be withdrawn.

The Fifteenth Amendment (1870) made it impossible simply to disfranchise blacks, so the Bourbons devised other, less direct, means to keep them from voting. They instituted a poll tax that most blacks could not afford to pay and literacy tests that most blacks, and many whites, could not pass.

Mississippi led the way in the disfranchisement of blacks. At a state convention held in 1890, delegates modified the Reconstruction constitution of 1868, which had extended suffrage to blacks. First, Mississippi established a new residency requirement of two years in the state and one year in the election district that often prevented both black and white tenant farmers, who habitually moved every year, from voting. Second, the new provisions disqualified voters convicted of certain crimes such as vagrancy, to which blacks were uncommonly susceptible. Third, the reforms mandated that all taxes, including the poll tax, be paid by 1 February of election year. Even those rare blacks who could afford to pay their taxes either moved frequently or were not in the habit of keeping careful records.

They had plenty of time to lose tax receipts before election day arrived in the fall and were thus barred from voting. Fourth, the new regulations instituted a literacy test. To assist illiterate whites who could not, for example, read a passage from the Constitution, most Southern states instituted what became known as the "understanding clause." An election official read a portion of the Constitution to a potential white voter and then asked if he had understood it. If he answered "yes," he was permitted to vote.

Other states found different ways for whites to get around the literacy requirement. In 1895 the South Carolina legislature declared that owning property assessed at $300 qualified an illiterate voter. Many more whites than blacks met the prerequisite. Three years later the Louisiana state legislature invented the ingenious "grandfather clause," which enabled illiterates to vote if their fathers or grandfathers had been eligible on 1 January 1867, when all blacks in the state had been disfranchised. By 1910 the legislatures of Oklahoma, Alabama, Georgia, North Carolina, and Virginia had incorporated the grandfather clause into state election laws. Such restrictions were effective in limiting the black vote. In 1896, for example, 130,000 blacks registered to vote in Louisiana; by 1900 that number had fallen to 5,320. According to the census of 1900, Alabama had 121,259 literate black men over the age of twenty-one, all of whom ought to have been eligible to vote; only 3,742 were registered.

The federal government did little to rectify the situation. In 1890 the Senate, apparently not wishing to interfere in the internal affairs of the states, defeated a bill sponsored by Representative Henry Cabot Lodge (R.-Mass.) that would have authorized federal supervision of state elections to reexamine the qualifications of those excluded from voting. Lodge's bill marked the last significant attempt to protect black voters until Congress passed the Voting Rights Act (1965).

THE STATUS OF CIVIL RIGHTS

Despite their political limitations, blacks won a few major, if short-lived, victories, chief among them passage of the Civil

Rights Act (1875). Although poorly enforced, the Act outlawed discrimination in transportation, theaters, restaurants, hotels, and other places of public accommodation. In 1883, however, the U.S. Supreme Court ruled, with only one dissent, that the Fourteenth Amendment (1868) prohibited state governments from discriminating on the basis of race but did not restrict private organizations, companies, or individuals from doing so. Hence, railroad and street-car companies, restaurants, hotels, theaters, private clubs, hospitals, and the like could legally keep blacks out if they wished.

The repeal of the Civil Rights Act of 1875 did not immediately rob blacks of their rights any more than its passage had guaranteed them. In 1885, for instance, blacks in South Carolina continued to ride in first-class railway cars apparently without exciting comment. As early as 1881, by contrast, the Tennessee state legislature had required railroads operating in the state to provide separate first-class cars for blacks and whites. Not until 1888 did Mississippi require separate railway cars for blacks and whites. When in 1890 Louisiana also established separate cars for blacks and whites, Homer Plessy, an octoroon (one-eighth black) convicted for refusing to leave an all-white car, challenged the constitutionality of the law in the U.S. Supreme Court.

The justices rendered their decision in the case of *Plessy v. Ferguson* in 1896, upholding state laws that mandated segregation. Writing the majority opinion, Justice Henry Brown Billings from Massachusetts declared that segregation laws "have been generally, if not universally, recognized as within the competency of state legislatures in the exercise of their police power." Separate seating arrangements, the majority of the Court concluded, thus did not deprive blacks of their constitutional rights. The sole dissenting voice came from Justice John Marshall Harlan, a former slaveholder and Unionist from Kentucky, who had also opposed repeal of the Civil Rights Act of 1875. "In my opinion," Harlan wrote, "the judgment this day rendered will, in time, prove to be quite as pernicious as the decision made by this tribunal in the Dred Scott Case." The ruling, Harlan predicted, would "stimulate aggressions, more or less brutal, upon the admitted rights of colored citizens."

Events made Harlan's words prophetic. Soon the principle of segregation extended to every aspect of life for blacks, from public accommodations to recreation and sports to health care and employment. The violence that Justice Harlan had foretold also became a reality. Between 1890 and 1899 the number of lynchings that occurred in the United States averaged 187.5 per year, 82 percent of which took place in the South. In 1892 black journalist and social activist Ida B. Wells launched what eventually became an international movement opposed to lynching when she wrote a series of articles about the lynching of three friends in Memphis, Tennessee. The antilynching movement attracted considerable support in all regions of the United States, including the South, much of it coming from white women. Wells's goal was the enactment of a federal antilynching law, which would empower the U.S. government to prosecute those responsible for lynchings when local and state governments failed or refused to do so.

The opposition to lynching, however, was an exception to the general support for white supremacy. Few whites, Northern or Southern, ever fully accepted the idea of racial equality with former slaves. In time, Northerners who feared the invasion of blacks into their states became increasingly sympathetic to the view of Southerners that black equality really meant the oppression of white people. The reality that blacks faced in both the North and the South during the last thirty years of the nineteenth century was the emergence of a racial caste system embodied in the laws of the United States and sustained by the attitudes and conduct of whites. Regrettably, the hopes that the majority of black Americans had long entertained for equality and integration remained unfulfilled.

CHRONOLOGY

1619

African slaves arrive in America in Jamestown, Virginia, the first of thousands of Africans brought to America in bondage during the seventeenth century.

1638

Slavery takes root in Massachusetts Bay Colony. The Massachusetts code of laws is the first colonial legal code to mention slavery.

1700

Samuel Sewall, a Massachusetts magistrate, publishes *The Selling of Joseph*, the oldest surviving American antislavery document. Sewall writes in response to another judge, John Saffin, who kept a black indentured servant in bondage after his indentureship had expired.

1754

John Woolman, a New Jersey Quaker, publishes *Some Considerations on the Keeping of Negroes*, an antislavery tract. The Quakers become vocal abolitionists.

1775

An abolition society is established in Philadelphia by Quakers.

1776

The Continental Congress issues the Declaration of Independence, asserting the American colonies' independence from Great Britain. The opening statement in the document asserts that "all men are created equal" and that they possess "certain unalienable rights," including "life, liberty, and the pursuit of

happiness." An antislavery clause is opposed by southern delegates and stricken from an early draft of the Declaration.

1783

The American colonies gain their independence from Great
Britain. Slavery remains in place after the American Revolution.

1787

Congress passes the Northwest Ordinance, banning slavery in
northwestern territories owned by the United States. American slavery is a subject of debate at the Philadelphia Convention of 1787, which results in the creation of the U.S. Constitution.

1788

U.S. Constitution is ratified. The document guarantees the return of fugitive slaves, allows the importation of slaves for
twenty years, and considers slaves as three-fifths of a person for
the purpose of counting a state's population.

1793

Eli Whitney patents the cotton gin. Southern cotton, which is
planted, tended, and harvested by slaves, becomes the South's
king crop.

1794

The first national abolition society in the United States, the
American Convention for the Promotion of the Abolition of
Slavery, is established in Philadelphia.

1800

Gabriel Prosser, a Virginia blacksmith, initiates a slave rebellion
in Virginia. The rebellion is quickly suppressed, and Prosser and
his conspirators are hanged.

1808

Congress outlaws the importation of slaves into the United States. The maximum sentence for violating this law is the death penalty.

1820

Congress passes the Missouri Compromise, which allows Missouri to enter the Union as a slave state and Maine to enter as a free state. The Missouri legislation also prohibits slavery in U.S. territories north of latitude 36°30' north.

1822

Denmark Vesey, a former slave living in South Carolina, plans a slave rebellion but is betrayed before his plan can unfold. He is arrested and executed.

1827

The first abolitionist newspaper managed by African Americans, *Freedom's Journal*, is established.

1829

David Walker, an African American freeman, publishes *David Walker's Appeal*, a militant antislavery pamphlet.

1831

On January 1, William Lloyd Garrison publishes the first edition of the *Liberator*. This antislavery newspaper will continue its weekly publication until slavery is abolished in 1865. In August, Nat Turner, a Virginia slave, ignites a slave rebellion that takes the lives of sixty white people. Turner is eventually captured and hanged. After Turner's death an attorney who interviewed him publishes *The Confessions of Nat Turner*.

1833

Garrison and other leading abolitionists establish the American Anti-Slavery Society in Philadelphia.

1837

Elijah Lovejoy, the editor of an abolitionist newspaper, is murdered by a proslavery mob that attacks his newspaper office in Alton, Illinois.

1839

Theodore D. Weld publishes his influential antislavery text *American Slavery as It Is*. Illegally imported slaves aboard the ship *Amistad* stage a mutiny. Former president John Quincy Adams argues their case before the U.S. Supreme Court and gains the slaves an acquittal.

1840

The antislavery Liberty Party is formed. The party runs candidates in the 1840 and 1844 presidential elections.

1841

Lydia Maria Child becomes the editor of the *National Anti-Slavery Standard*, the newspaper of the American Anti-Slavery Society.

1845

Frederick Douglass publishes his first autobiography, *Narrative of the Life of Frederick Douglass, an American Slave*. Douglass joins Garrison and becomes a key figure in the abolitionist movement. The United States wages war with Mexico. After the war Texas joins the Union as a slave state.

1847

Douglass establishes the *North Star*, an abolitionist newspaper.

1849

Harriet Tubman escapes from slavery in Maryland. She becomes active in the Underground Railroad, a network of hiding places for runaway slaves.

1850

Congress passes the Compromise of 1850, which allows California to enter the Union as a free state, outlaws the trading of slaves in Washington, D.C., and enacts a strict Fugitive Slave Law.

1851

Harriet Beecher Stowe begins serializing the story of a fictional slave named Uncle Tom in the *National Era*, an abolitionist newspaper. The following year the story is published in novel form as *Uncle Tom's Cabin*. The book becomes an enormous best seller and the most effective piece of abolitionist writing.

1854

Congress passes the Kansas-Nebraska Act, which negates the Missouri Compromise by allowing the citizens in the Kansas and Nebraska territories to vote on the slavery issue before entering the Union. Abolitionists are outraged by the prospect of slavery spreading to territories identified as free by the Missouri Compromise. The Republican Party is formed. It pledges to halt the spread of American slavery.

1857

The U.S. Supreme Court decides the *Dred Scott* case. Scott, a Missouri slave, remains in bondage even though his owner had taken him to live in free territory.

1859

John Brown leads an unsuccessful slave revolt in Harpers Ferry, Virginia. He is captured, found guilty of murder and treason, and hanged. Abolitionists hail Brown as a martyr.

1860

Republican Abraham Lincoln is elected president. He gains the presidency on a platform of no extension of slavery into new states and territories. In the wake of Lincoln's election several southern states vote to secede from the Union. In his inaugural address Lincoln promises the South that he has no intention of trying to abolish slavery.

1861

The Civil War begins. President Lincoln maintains that the war is being fought to restore the Union, not to abolish slavery.

1862

In September Lincoln issues the Preliminary Emancipation Proclamation, informing the South that he intends to free the slaves in the rebellious states on January 1, 1863.

1863

On January 1, Lincoln issues the Emancipation Proclamation freeing the slaves in states that have seceded from the Union.

1865

In January Congress approves the Thirteenth Amendment to the United States Constitution, which makes slavery illegal throughout the United States. In December the requisite number of states ratify the amendment, making it a part of the Constitution. In April the Civil War ends, and Lincoln is assassinated.

1868

The Fourteenth Amendment to the U.S. Constitution is enacted. It makes all persons born in the United States citizens, including former slaves.

FOR FURTHER RESEARCH

Primary Documents

Larry Ceplair, ed., *The Public Years of Sarah and Angelina Grimké: Selected Writings, 1835–1839*. New York: Columbia University Press, 1989.

Frederick Douglass, *Narrative of the Life of Frederick Douglass, an American Slave*. Garden City, NY: Anchor, 1973.

William Dudley, ed., *Slavery: Opposing Viewpoints*. San Diego: Greenhaven, 1992.

George M. Fredrickson, ed., *William Lloyd Garrison*. Englewood Cliffs, NJ: Prentice-Hall, 1968.

Henry Louis Gates Jr., ed., *The Classic Slave Narratives*. New York: New American Library, 1987.

Joanne Grant, ed., *Black Protest: History, Documents, and Analyses, 1619 to the Present*. New York: Fawcett, 1968.

Kenneth S. Greenberg, ed., *The Confessions of Nat Turner and Related Documents*. Boston: Bedford, 1996.

Robert W. Johannsen, ed., *Reconstruction, 1865–1877*. New York: Free Press, 1970.

Abraham Lincoln, *Selected Speeches and Writings*. New York: Vintage, 1992.

Richard A. Long, ed., *Black Writers and the Civil War*. Secaucus, NJ: Blue and Grey, 1988.

Mason Lowance, ed., *Against Slavery: An Abolitionist Reader*. New York: Penguin, 2000.

Louis P. Masur, ed., *"The Real War Will Never Get in the Books": Selections from Writers During the Civil War*. New York: Oxford University Press, 1993.

Donald G. Matthews, ed., *Agitation for Freedom: The Abolitionist Movement*. New York: John Wiley, 1972.

Eric L. McKitrick, ed., *Slavery Defended: The Views of the Old South*. Englewood Cliffs, NJ: Prentice-Hall, 1963.

William H. Pease and Jane H. Pease, eds., *The Antislavery Argument*. Indianapolis: Bobbs–Merrill, 1965.

Louis Ruchames, ed., *A John Brown Reader*. London: Abelard-Shuman, 1959.

Harriet Beecher Stowe, *Uncle Tom's Cabin*. New York: W.W. Norton, 1994.

Charles M. Wiltse, ed., *David Walker's Appeal, in Four Articles*. New York: Hill and Wang, 1965.

Histories and Biographies

Herbert Aptheker, *American Negro Slave Revolts*. New York: International Publishers, 1965.

Ira Berlin, *Many Thousands Gone: The First Two Centuries of Slavery in North America*. Cambridge, MA: Harvard University Press, 1998.

David W. Blight, *Frederick Douglass's Civil War: Keeping Faith in Jubilee*. Baton Rouge: Louisiana State University Press, 1989.

LaWanda Cox, *Lincoln and Black Freedom: A Study of Presidential Leadership*. Columbia: University of South Carolina Press, 1981.

Merton L. Dillon, *The Abolitionists: The Growth of a Dissenting Minority*. DeKalb: Northern Illinois University Press, 1974.

Martin Duberman, ed., *The Antislavery Vanguard*. Princeton, NJ: Princeton University Press, 1965.

Dwight Lowell Dumond, *Antislavery: The Crusade for Freedom in America*. New York: W.W. Norton, 1961.

Don E. Fehrenbacher, *Prelude to Greatness: Lincoln in the 1850s.* Stanford, CA: Stanford University Press, 1962.

Eric Foner, *Free Soil, Free Labor, Free Men.* New York: Oxford University Press, 1970.

———, *Nothing but Freedom: Emancipation and Its Legacy.* Baton Rouge: Louisiana State University Press, 1983.

———, *Reconstruction: America's Unfinished Revolution, 1863–1877.* New York: Harper & Row, 1988.

———, *Slavery, the Civil War, and Reconstruction.* Washington, DC: American Historical Association, 1990.

John Hope Franklin, *The Emancipation Proclamation.* Garden City, NY: Doubleday, 1963.

———, *From Slavery to Freedom: A History of African Americans.* Boston: McGraw-Hill, 2000.

———, *Reconstruction: After the Civil War.* Chicago: University of Chicago Press, 1961.

Lawrence Friedman, *Gregarious Saints: Self and Community in American Abolitionism, 1830–1870.* New York: Cambridge University Press, 1982.

Allen C. Guelzo, *Abraham Lincoln: Redeemer President.* Grand Rapids, MI: William B. Eerdmans, 1999.

Stanley Harrold, *The Rise of Aggressive Abolitionism.* Lexington: University Press of Kentucky, 2004.

Joan Hedrick, *Harriet Beecher Stowe: A Life.* New York: Oxford University Press, 1994.

Peter P. Hinks, *To Awaken My Afflicted Burden: David Walker and the Problem of Antebellum Slave Resistance.* University Park: Pennsylvania State University Press, 1996.

Nathan Irwin Huggins, *Slave and Citizen: The Life of Frederick Douglass.* Boston: Little, Brown, 1980.

Stanley I. Kutler, ed., *The* Dred Scott *Decision: Law and Politics.* Boston: Houghton Mifflin, 1967.

Leon F. Litwack, *Been in the Storm So Long: The Aftermath of Slavery.* New York: Vintage, 1980.

Henry Mayer, *All on Fire: William Lloyd Garrison and the Abolition of Slavery.* New York: St. Martin's, 1998.

James M. McPherson, *Battle Cry of Freedom: The Civil War Era.* New York: Oxford University Press, 1988.

Edmund Morgan, *American Slavery, American Freedom.* New York: W.W. Norton, 1975.

Stephen B. Oates, *Our Fiery Trial: Abraham Lincoln, John Brown, and the Civil War.* Amherst: University of Massachusetts Press, 1979.

Benjamin Quarles, *The Black Abolitionists.* New York: Oxford University Press, 1969.

———, *Lincoln and the Negro.* New York: Oxford University Press, 1962.

Leonard L. Richards, *The Slave Power: The Free North and Southern Domination, 1780–1860.* Baton Rouge: Louisiana State University Press, 2000.

Dorothy Schneider, *Slavery in America: From Colonial Times to the Civil War.* New York: Facts On File, 2000.

James B. Stewart, *Holy Warriors.* New York: Hill and Wang, 1976.

James Tackach, *The Abolition of American Slavery.* San Diego: Lucent, 2002.

———, *Lincoln's Moral Vision: The Second Inaugural Address.* Jackson: University Press of Mississippi, 2002.

Geoffrey C. Ward, Ric Burns, and Ken Burns, *The Civil War: An Illustrated History.* New York: Alfred A. Knopf, 1990.

INDEX

North, the
call for secession by, 31
economy of, 17–18, 72,
79–80, 214
emancipation in, 16, 17, 72
slave trade abolished in, 51
North Carolina, 93–94, 196,
197, 199
North Star (newspaper), 26
Notes on the State of Virginia
(Jefferson), 74

Observer (newspaper), 24
Otis, James, 50–51

Paine, Thomas, 51
Parker, Theodore, 25
Paul, Thomas, 107–108
Peak, John, 107
Pennsylvania, 14, 16, 72
Pennsylvania Abolition
Society, 71
Phillips, Wendell, 35, 185
Pierce, Franklin, 28
Pinckney, Charles, 78, 80
plantation society, 18–19,
194, 200–201, 211
"Plea for Captain John
Brown, A" (Thoreau), 32
Plessy v. Ferguson (1896),
217–18
politics
black, after Civil War,
193–201, 202–203
racism in southern, 214–15
Slave Power and, 28
using, to end slavery, 30–31
women and, 25
see also Democratic Party;
Republican Party

poll taxes, 215–16
"popular sovereignty," 28
Populist/People's Party,
214–15
"Prayer of Twenty Millions,
The" (Greeley), 154
property rights
compensation to
slaveholders and, 87
in *Dred Scott* case, 30
as natural rights, 74
public transportation,
217–18
Puritans, 14, 15, 16, 39–44,
46

Quakers, 14, 16, 18, 46–53,
73, 122
Quincy, Edmund, 192

racism
belief in inferiority of
Africans and, 51–52
Black Codes and, 210–12
during colonial era, 41–42
contradicts democratic
principles, 198
laws cannot overcome,
87–88
national identity and, 74
segregation and, 210,
216–18
used by southern white
politicians, 214–15
use of, in history, 188–89
violence and, 212–14,
217–18
Rapier, James T., 196
rebellions, slave
in ancient history, 57–58